The Power
In You

The Power
In You

How to Accept Your Past, Live in the

Present and Shape a Positive Future

HENRY FRASER

First published in Great Britain in 2020 by Orion Spring
an imprint of The Orion Publishing Group Ltd
Carmelite House, 50 Victoria Embankment
London EC4Y 0DZ

An Hachette UK Company

1 3 5 7 9 10 8 6 4 2

A CIP catalogue record for this book is
available from the British Library.

ISBN: HB 978 1 8418 8336 6
eBook 978 1 8418 8338 0

Typeset by Born Group
Printed and bound in Great Britain by Clays Ltd, Elcograf S.p.A.

www.orionbooks.co.uk

This book is for my friends and family who have been with me and tirelessly supported me since day one. Everything I do I dedicate to you.

Foreword by Fearne Cotton

THANK GOODNESS YOU picked up this book. Thank goodness you know about, or are about to get to know, Henry Fraser.

I first heard about Henry's story from a friend at my publishing house. She told me I would love his outlook on life and also his art work. Being a lover of learning and paint, I was instantly intrigued. I read Henry's first book, *The Little Big Things*, in two days. Mouth wide open, I raced through the story of how

Henry learned to live life in a totally new, challenging way with such grace and unbelievable strength. It made me look at my own life in interesting ways. I was first struck by how floored I can be by silly minor challenges, but also inspired to think I must have a deeper strength in me somewhere too. I had to meet him.

The next step was to follow Henry on Instagram, study his style of painting, and then slide in to his DMs to suss whether he fancied coming on the Happy Place podcast. He said yes. Phew! Arriving at Henry's house I sensed such a Zen-like calm emitting from him, and I hung off his every word. This was a true pioneer, living a happy life in the face of extreme physical adversity. Here was someone willing to open their heart and soul to offer up story-telling and thoughts around a very tough personal time. Here was an activist making as much noise as he could about creating equality for disabled people. I massively appreciate Henry's wisdom on the podcast as I learned a hell of a lot from it – and I know my listeners did too.

I get nervous during my podcasts as I care so much that the guest enjoys the experience and that I get the best from them and their story. I don't want to say anything that could cause upset or be triggering, so I thought carefully about how I might talk to Henry about his accident and life thereafter. The thing is, I didn't need to. One of Henry's most brilliant qualities is that you can ask him anything. He wants his answers to give relief and understanding to people who aren't in the same position. He wants to tell his story.

This book is filled with answers. So many brilliant answers to questions you may, yourself, want to ask Henry. Questions you might feel worried to ask, and some you genuinely need to know the answer to as you think it could help you too. This is a book about life and how to adapt to the ever-changing winds we experience on a daily basis. Although Henry has experienced extreme and very instant change in his life, all of Henry's thoughts and answers can be applied to the challenges we face in everyday life.

The Power In You is a practical book because Henry's own story allows us to see what we are capable of, and how we might achieve more personal mental flexibility and agility. Henry has so many big plans – some you'll read about in this book – and you will undoubtedly feel excited uncovering what possibilities might lie on the horizon for you too. Henry is all about expansion, challenges and giving things a go, and we all need a little inspiration when it comes to that. Henry is an inspiring soul, so you'll definitely feel energised and motivated by what he has to say.

I can see Henry now shaking his head as I call him an inspiration as he doesn't see himself that way at all. The best people usually don't! You will, though; whether Henry likes it or not, you won't be able to escape being greatly inspired by his words. He proves that big life challenges don't lead to giving up your dreams. He shows that by telling stories we can unite and create positive change. He demonstrates how being creative can bring such depth to your life. This is an opportunity for us all to explore our own strengths and how we can navigate the unexpected. Get your questions about life ready, as Henry has the answers.

Introduction

I KNOW YOU have a question in your head, one that if we met in person, you might be too shy or too uncomfortable to ask. Maybe you think it would be rude to say the words out loud, too personal or too searching for me.

But if you were to ask me a question, what would it be? In the ten years since my accident I've been asked a lot of questions, but at the heart of every one lies the same sentiment: what's it like to be paralysed?

What's it like to live this life, one that I didn't expect, one that many may think is catastrophically restricted?

For those of you who don't know my story, at the age of seventeen I experienced a freak accident that left me paralysed, unable to walk or move or feel anything from the shoulders down. On a summer holiday with my friends in Portugal, I dived into the sea and hit my head on a submerged sandbank. In danger of drowning, I moved my head to the side to get some air and in that split second severely crushed my spinal cord. After many months of operations, life-threatening infections, physio, rehabilitation and much grit and determination, I returned home to face a totally different life to the one I had lived before. Life since has been filled with adversity and challenge, but with a good deal of adventure and happiness along the way.

Adventure? Happiness? But I can't walk, I can't move anything below my shoulders. How can that be? I am often asked. Well, ten years after my accident, I can honestly say that the limitations of my physical movement directly correlate to the expansion of my world. In these years I have discovered so much about myself. My world is bigger now than it ever was, my relationships are stronger, and I have so much to look forward to.

The greatest challenges I have faced may not be the ones you'd expect. But one thing that has become clear to me is that we all face challenges, every day. Challenges that increase our anxiety, that disconnect us from the people we love, that make our world smaller. But those challenges can also open up our world in unexpected ways.

From the hardest moments I have discovered the most precious of all facts: the power to deal with adversity is in you.

Sometimes you may need a little help to tap into that internal strength, but I truly believe that it's there in all of us. I have to be honest here. I'm not a big one for giving out advice. I'm also uncomfortable with the label 'inspiration', but I know that my experience has given me genuine insights into what matters in life. Insights that have helped me confront my greatest fears, to truly live in the present and look at the future with great hope and expectation.

When I give talks about what happened to me and how I have adapted to my new life, I always leave time for questions from the audience. For many, it's the first time they have ever been in a room with someone who has no movement from the shoulders downwards. Rather than just hear my scripted talk, I want them to be able to ask me anything that springs to mind. Nothing is off limits – within reason, of course. I am a great believer in asking questions and listening to answers so that we can better understand each other. Given the opportunity to enlighten or share what it's like being in my situation, beyond what I cover in my talk, I am always up for answering any questions.

As you will see from the questions and answers that follow, they get right to the heart of what it's like being me. Having done these question-and-answer sessions for some years now, I've learned that what lies behind the questions is a sense of wonder at how I find the will to go on when circumstances are difficult. I have come to realise that this is not just a question for me, the young man in the wheelchair – it's a question for all of us. We all face challenges or adversity – changes in circumstances, accidents, illness or shifts that unsettle us – and we all have to deal with them.

My challenges are just more obvious to the outside world because they're more visible. Your challenges may be different, but they will feel no less overwhelming to you. My experience has made me think deeply about the power in all of us to effect change, to feel hopeful and to live our best lives.

This book has emerged from those question-and-answer sessions. It's my attempt to share what I've learned – what I am *still* learning. Because as a result of my life-changing accident, I now see that sharing our challenges, and the way we use the power within us, helps us all.

1

What do you *do* all day?

WHEN I WAS first asked 'What do you do all day?' the questioner – a ten-year-old pupil at a school I was visiting – couldn't help but put some heavy emphasis on the second do. 'What do you *do* all day?' he asked, voicing his – and many others' – genuine belief that because I am disabled, I can't actually *do* much at all. Because I can no longer walk or move my arms, because I need twenty-four-hour care, while I may still be *living* each day, I can't be said to be *doing*.

Fair. At the talk my mum had been sitting beside me. She'd wheeled me in, scrolled through my iPad as I referenced my speaking notes, and when my mouth had gone dry, she'd put a straw in my mouth so I could drink.

That little boy was asking the question a lot of people would like to ask but are either too polite or too frightened to put into words. They would like to know what it's like to be me, mainly because they can't imagine being totally dependent on others. Maybe it conjures up indescribable horror and indignity, maybe they picture endless hours of inactivity and boredom, day after dark-blue day filled with introspection. This is understandable; these may well have been my unspoken questions for a tetraplegic before I became one. It can be a strange experience to feel that you are effectively living someone else's worst nightmare, but the truth is that we are all capable of adapting to circumstances that may once have felt impossible. If you had asked me ten years ago how I would feel being paraplegic, I would have told you that it would be the worst thing I could imagine. And yet here I am, living a life that I love.

Certainly, there are moments when I wish I could go to the toilet without being helped. And there are moments when I'd like to be able to eat without someone feeding me. Of course there are days when I'd like to hop on the tube and go into town, alone. But over the years these have become fleeting desires, things I don't pay much attention to. I need to go the loo – I need help. I need to eat – I have to be fed. If I need to go into town, I get a cab – just like you may. I have found that people's questions for the disabled are so focused on the functional – how do you eat, how do you shave, how do you get around. But I have come to see that life is about so much more than the functional. It's much richer and larger in scope; there is so much to appreciate, so much to become involved in, so much to be thankful for. Whether I can tie my own shoelaces or not makes no difference to the quality or purpose of my life. It may have taken my accident and a great big shift in mindset to get here, but here I am. What may surprise you is that I don't mind being asked about it.

So I suppose I should answer the question, just as I did for that ten-year-old. How does a day in my life as a tetraplegic pan out? Well, as you will see, much of it is taken up with functionality – at a level that an able-bodied person might never consider – but there's also a hefty dose of normality: work, friends, social media, adventure. To paraphrase Barack Obama: the sun will rise in the morning whether you are able-bodied or disabled. It's the same sun, it's the same day.

✷

SO, HOW DO my days look? Well, pretty different to yours in some ways, but surprisingly similar in others. It begins with one of my carers coming into my bedroom around 7.15 a.m. to open the blinds. As the light streams in, while I adjust to waking up, she crosses my legs and feet. Because I've been lying flat all night without moving, my body could kick out when touched – a sort of involuntary spasm. Adjusting the bed to a sitting position and moving my legs as soon as I wake up helps prevent that. After my accident it took a while to adjust to the shock of waking up each morning to find myself completely dependent on others – to sit me up, to wash me, to dress me, to feed and water me – but now this is as natural as night following day.

My bedroom has been adapted to take account of my needs. I sleep on a profiling bed that can be adjusted according to whether I need to sit or lie down, and to a height that is comfortable for my carers. My parents had the carpet replaced with lino so my wheelchair can glide across a smooth surface, and the en-suite bathroom (this had been my older brother Tom's bedroom – he got all the luxuries growing up) was converted into a wet room. I am also fortunate that we could afford to install air conditioning; controlling my temperature is something I need to be on top of throughout the day. It never would have occurred to me to be grateful for my body's ability to regulate its own temperature before I lost that ability, but it is now just a part of my life to take steps to manage it.

I also have some pieces of essential kit in my room: a standing chair, so I can stretch my limbs, plus my trusty hoist to lift me in and out of bed.

Maybe to you this all sounds horribly clinical; you're picturing my bedroom as some sort of hospital room – but it isn't. I have a TV, pictures, posters, books, cuddly toys from my childhood on a favourite old armchair . . . There are plenty of things around me that make the room feel homely and lovely to be in. It's a real sanctuary for me. The equipment and adaptations provide enormous comfort that make my daily life so much easier. In the summer, everyone wants to be up in my room to take advantage of the air conditioning, as mine is the only room in the house that has it. This comes in handy when I need to extract favours from my family.

The first task of the day is to take my medication. It may come as a surprise to you, but I don't need anything other than ascorbic acid, to give me added vitamin C, and oxybutynin, to keep my bladder relaxed during the day. The bladder is a muscle, and like every other muscle in my body, it's liable to spasm – but contractions there would cause me considerably more trouble than the odd twitch in any of my other muscles. My carer places the pills on my tongue and while I swallow them down, she empties the urine bag from the side of my bed. She then switches on the TV so I can check the local weather, which is something of an obsession. The conditions will dictate what I wear; dressing so I don't get too hot or too cold can make a real difference to my day.

Leaning me forward, she places the sling behind me, tucking it under my bum. She sits me back in it, straightens my legs and gets it into position so that, once in it, my weight is distributed as evenly as possible. She then clips me to the hoist – imagine a portable crane – to lower me into my shower chair. With this, the first of many adjustments of the day begins. Whenever and wherever I am sitting, I need to be as central as possible in the chair. If I'm even a fraction to one side or the other, I will have to lean in order to keep myself straight. While there's no exact science to it, over the years I have figured out how to fine-tune this procedure. So, I look left then right from the position I've landed in and tell my carer which way to shift me. It usually takes a few shimmies to one side, then the other, before I am in position. At this point she can wheel me into the bathroom and place my chair over the toilet. She'll leave me alone until I'm finished. Then, with my dignity intact, she wheels me into the shower and washes me, leaving my hair and face until last. I learned early on that, because I feel the cold so much, if we washed my hair and face first it meant I couldn't warm up afterwards, even under a hot shower.

Having someone so intimately involved with my body took some getting used to. From the moment of my accident, my body became the property of other people. I was constantly touched and manipulated by an army of doctors, nurses, physios and other members of the hospital team, as well as my immediate family. Even though I couldn't feel any of it below my shoulders, adapting to this has been one of the more challenging aspects of my situation.

By the time I finish my shower I'll have been awake about an hour and a quarter. Drying takes another twenty minutes or so. Every nook and cranny of my body needs to be dry, otherwise I may get sores, so my carer does this carefully and thoroughly. Then my hands and feet have to be moisturised as they get ridiculously dry due to the lack of blood flowing to my extremities. I have the silkiest hands of anyone this side of the M25, and I'm told my feet are enviably soft, which is definitely a long way from my mud-caked, cracked rugby feet of old.

Once the night urine bag has been taken off, my carer attaches a leg bag which is strapped to my calf. This lasts throughout the day, emptied at regular intervals. She then transfers me from the shower chair back into bed (think hoist and sling), puts the bed in a seated position, and arranges my body so I'm sitting forward with my legs stretched out in front of me. I'm now ready to choose what I am going to wear for the day.

I have a good line in hoodies – there is no denying that the hoods in my hoodies see plenty of action throughout the day, shifting up or down, depending on my level of warmth. Some have been with me for many years now, and I wouldn't part with them for anything. My carer lays my clothes out, leans the bed back so it's completely flat, then we get going. By this time, she has turned off the TV. I like to start the day chilled, so we put on Radio One. Depending on whether we're both in the mood, we might chat. Just as my carers respect my moods and needs, I try to respect theirs.

The most essential piece of clothing for me is my corset – which is not something I would have said ten years ago. I've worn one since my accident; initially to stop scoliosis (curvature of the spine) forming, then for balance and breathing. Because I have no working abdominals, the corset basically carries out the function of my abs, taking some of the strain off my diaphragm. Breathing would be incredibly tiring without the corset. Once it's been adjusted and secured accurately – being a tetraplegic takes a *lot* of patience, as these things rely on trial and error on a daily basis – on go my trousers and shoes. Then I am hoisted up, the sling placed under my legs so I can be lowered into my wheelchair, where I'll spend the next twelve or so hours. Once all the straightening and adjusting palaver is out of the way, on goes my T-shirt and hoodie. Finally I'm ready to go downstairs, where two cushions are placed on my lap and my hands are adjusted according to my obsessive need to have them positioned *exactly* the way I want them. This can test the mettle of my carers.

When I was discharged from hospital in February 2010, I had to spend the first couple of months at home sleeping in the kitchen because there was no way to get me upstairs to my bedroom. Having my own personal space has always been a priority, so this was a testing time for me. I found it hard, not being able to remove myself from the family and retreat to the sanctuary of my bedroom. It was hard for them too. There were times I could sense that my mum wanted to start cooking, or someone was desperate to make themselves a cup of tea, but they stayed out of the kitchen so I could have some temporary privacy. Thankfully, my parents had a lift installed for me, and it has been a true live-saver. When you are as dependent as I am on other people, being able to have privacy, a room that is yours alone (until you have to call your carer), is crucial for everyone's sanity.

Personal space is as important for the people around me as it is for me. My situation has given me an opportunity to observe what I need, and what others need, if we are to get along. One of the ways I have adapted to being in a wheelchair is by establishing some strong boundaries – and the ability to articulate those boundaries. Our own needs tend to sit on the back burner when we are rushing around being pulled in all directions by the demands of our lives. Taking time for ourselves might seem selfish. But only by establishing what your needs are, and prioritising them, can you give yourself a strong foundation from which to engage with the world.

By the time I'm wheeled into the living room, it's about 10.15 – getting me up, washed, dressed and downstairs takes about three hours. Now it's time for breakfast. I have to watch what I eat as I have so few opportunities to burn calories. When I first came home – after six weeks of being fed intravenously, followed by months spent retraining myself to swallow, living on hospital food – I couldn't get enough of the favourite meals that Mum and her mum – my yiayia – made in true Greek family tradition. Not to mention the bonus meals that friends and extended family plied us with. As a result, I put on heaps of weight that left me feeling uncomfortable in myself and so I have become much stricter, mastering the art of politely yet firmly refusing offers of food.

On Mondays I tend to skip breakfast because I will have eaten – and possibly drunk – too much over the weekend. But Tuesday to Thursday, I have a peppermint tea, yoghurt, granola and honey, or, once in a while, an avocado. Fridays are the big day as I usually do two hours of intense physio, so I need my carbs. That's the only time I allow myself my favourite treat: a toasted bagel with ham, cheese and caramelised onion. Perhaps because I've given up snacks, sweets, chocolate and cakes, I look forward to this bagel all week. I'd happily double the physio, or sell my wheelchair, before giving up my Friday bagel.

Everything I eat or drink has to be fed to me. It takes a few meals before any new carer can get the rhythm of my eating. Until we get it right, I can find myself having to chew much more quickly than I normally would, or waiting what seems like forever between mouthfuls. As a result, I've learned to be more confident in asking a carer to go faster, or wait a bit – much more straightforward than trying to adapt to a different speed of eating.

After breakfast, I go on my iPad to spend an hour or so reading and catching up with emails. I get lots of messages from people who've heard my story and want to tell me about their own situation or that of a loved one, and I like to respond to as many as possible. Technology is a wonderful thing; the sophistication and accuracy of my mouth stick, and the size of my iPad, enables me to communicate with relative ease. I value this time alone, but if I do need help there is always someone in the house who can come when I call. We use a series of sophisticated voice-activated baby monitors, which allow more privacy than the old ones that picked up the slightest sound, alerting my carer when I didn't actually need them.

On days when I'm painting, I call for my carer at midday, so she can set me up at my easel. Again, this requires some careful aligning. The wheelchair I use isn't suited to my level of disability; it doesn't have a headrest or armrests, which means it takes constant effort to maintain my balance while seated in it. That was a conscious choice I made early on in my rehab; over the years, I've worked long and hard at physio to remain capable of sitting in it. I love the lightness of that chair, and the slimline dimension of it. These things make a huge difference to my mobility, my freedom to be out and about. Whoever is pushing me can navigate me quite easily – believe me, when I'm on a night out with my friends, maybe indulging in a few too many, knowing they don't have to expend too much energy on pushing me or carrying me up or down stairs is pretty comforting.

My easel is at the table in our living room. Since I took up painting, my workspace has been honed to meet my needs. Mostly I need light and to be able to access my paints myself. My carer wheels me over to the table, places the brush in the mouth stick and sets the clamp in the right position. Then begins another session of aligning me in the chair, and the chair in relation to the easel. I need to be in the most comfortable position possible as I will be sitting there painting for hours.

Once we've got this right, my carer places a cloth over both arms so I can reach down with my mouth stick and wipe my brush on them. She spreads additional cloths on the floor to prevent paint splatter. Then, depending on what I'm painting, I choose the colours I need squeezed on to my palette. If I need photos or images for the painting, I'll have one set up on the cardboard next to the easel and one on the table, so I can turn both ways to look at it. It's taken years to calibrate the set-up so that my shoulders and neck don't hurt too much from the strain of painting.

This process may take fifteen minutes or so, but once I am set up, and the music I have chosen is turned on, that's it for a while. My carer will check on me every hour to see if my leg bag needs emptying or I need a drink or adjusting, but apart from that I'm on my own.

Around mid-afternoon, I have to stop. I've learned the hard way that to carry on for too long would place strain on my back and shoulders. When I call my carer, she wheels me back to the sofa area of the living room and sets me up on the iPad. I'm currently trying to learn Spanish; languages were never my thing at school, so I've set myself the challenge of improving. After half an hour of that, I'll answer any emails or tweets that have come in. After an hour or so, I need to rest a bit or else the combination of being close to my painting all afternoon and being on the iPad can make me a bit cross-eyed. Instead I relax by watching TV, kind of shutting my brain down until it's time to eat.

I never have lunch, so by five-thirty I'm hungry. I've been trying to reduce my meat intake by switching to pulses and beans, so I'm fortunate that my mum is an adaptable cook. My refusal to eat more is baffling to her – at times it's taken as much force of will to stop her popping in with tempting nutritious snacks throughout the day as it has to complete my most challenging physio reps. Supper, though, is something I relish. Mum always makes me a filling and nutritious meal, which I appreciate hugely.

Both Mum and Dad are around in the evenings, and my brothers will often come by, sometimes with their partners. Back in the early days after my accident, my brothers went out of their way to be at home or drop in to see me, to spend time with me. As the years have gone by they've married or moved out, but we're still extremely close. The fact that we've now settled into a more normal, less enmeshed way of life suits me well.

Depending on who is or isn't around, I might chat to them a bit or we might watch some sport. Before I began filling my days with speaking engagements, and painting for commissions or exhibitions, I used to be confined to the house a lot. So I'd be desperate to hear everyone's news, lapping up any gossip or details of life on the outside: what they'd been up to, who said what to who and where. Now, I'm so adept at using my phone and iPad, I can be in touch with my brothers and friends whenever I want, so the flow of communication is constant. Instead of sitting round talking, I tend to crave peace and quiet towards the end of the day. By 9 p.m. I'm exhausted. After twelve or so hours in my chair, I need to relax my body, come out of my corset and wind down.

On days when I've stayed at home painting, I am much less tired than I would be after giving a talk somewhere, or attending a physio session, or using my standing wheelchair or exercise bike. I'm usually at my most tired after a weekend spent with my friends. Getting out of the house is much less difficult than it used to be, mostly because my carers or family are much more confident about it, but I try to conserve energy by staying in bed longer beforehand, or going back to bed for a rest after exercise.

Like getting up in the morning, the process of getting into bed is also pretty time-consuming. My carer takes me upstairs, gets the sling and hoist ready, puts me on the bed in an upright position, undresses me, takes off the leg bag, attaches my night bag, puts a sheet and blanket over me, places cushions on my lap and sets up my iPad. For the next hour I'll chat with my mates online or float around social media. When my carer comes back in, she reclines the bed so I'm in a resting position, folds my pillow in half and puts it behind my head. I'll watch TV for half an hour – something I've watched before, nothing too taxing. This is the time I relax. Around 11 p.m., my carer comes in to lie me flat and take my pillow away. She then positions a rolled-up towel on each side of my head to stop it from moving too much in the night, as this can make my neck stiff and sore the next morning. I get thirsty in the night so, before leaving me to sleep, she places within reach of my mouth an extendable straw attached to a water jug. This is the penultimate ritualised adjustment of the day, after which she checks that my sheets and blanket are in place, then leaves me to it.

If I have been out giving a talk or attending a meeting, or have had an extreme physio session, I will be physically and mentally exhausted. Those nights, I fall asleep straight away. Other nights, it takes me longer. I have learned, over the years, to train my mind to think calmly, even if I'm thinking about something I may have reacted negatively to during the day. I like to take this time to work things out in a measured way. I may not be in control of most of my body, but I am in control of my mind, and I like to go to sleep with a clear mind.

I have come to appreciate that clear-mind feeling. Before my accident, I was inclined to be a worrier. Actually, I was a big worrier, forever anticipating 'what if', 'what when' . . . Often I would choose not to do things in case they didn't work out. I guess this changed because I had no choice. When you are thrown head first into a new situation, with no apparent way out, you have to focus on where you are in the moment. There is no longer a 'what if' to fret about – it's happened. You realise how fragile life is. For a time, I felt there was nothing left to anticipate, except maybe a real darkness. To shut that down, I learned to switch my mind's gears, to inhabit the present. We don't need to anticipate too far ahead. It is easier, more straightforward, to be in the moment. It took time to retrain my mind, but honestly, it was one of the best things I did.

Getting my temperature right during the night is an impossible feat. We have tried all sorts of heating and cooling devices, timers and voice-activated switches, but nothing seems to solve the problem. If I get too hot, I need the blanket taken off; too cold, I need the blanket, or another one, tucked in tighter. It's hard to ascertain which it will be. Rather than lose sleep worrying about it, I've reconciled myself to calling my carer during the night to adjust the blankets. With the voice-activated monitor, she can't hear me unless I call her, so if I don't need her for a few hours she can sleep uninterrupted.

✳

I HOPE THIS has gone some way to explaining what it is that I do *do* all day.

Describing my routine has brought home to me how much I now rely on others, which leads me to another question that I am asked a lot . . .

2

How did you cope with losing your independence?

BY FAR THE biggest change and challenge in my life, perhaps more so than my disability itself, is how much I depend on other people for my basic needs. Pre-accident, like most seventeen-year-olds, I *relied* on others to varying degrees. Post-accident, with a severely crushed spinal cord, my life has moved into a whole new dimension of dependence.

Ironically, the accident occurred on my first adult-free holiday abroad, just as I was crossing the brink of becoming more independent. I'd seen the benefits my two older brothers had enjoyed – learning to drive, staying out later with their friends – and I was ready for the same qualitative shift in freedom. Little did I know, as the sea came crashing over me, that I would be forced to do a complete about-turn and learn how to be more dependent.

Fortunately, my family has always been a source of emotional and practical support, each of us there for the others. The usual family stuff. The close relationship we share has made this much easier. We've always been a reasonably well-oiled team, depending on each other. Whatever the challenges – the ups and downs of being competitive rugby players or the death of members of the extended family – there's enough in the tank to get us through.

Will's recent marriage to my new sister-in-law, Sian, is a perfect illustration of how well we work together. From the stag weekend – and I mean a weekend of full-on stag – to the actual wedding itself, it was as if my care was one more part of the shared celebrations. This left me free to join in and be a part of it just like everyone else. For me, the privilege of close family is that I don't get treated like I have to be wrapped in cotton wool. My brothers tease me every bit as much as they ever did, though admittedly they are more gentle physically with me.

As I watched Will take his vows, sharing the joy of the occasion with the rest of my family, I was transported back to the moment when my brothers first saw me after the accident. Until then, it had been my parents by my bedside; the entire burden of care, the emotional weight of seeing me so helpless and broken, had fallen on them. Even in my fevered state, I was stricken by how much they were having to go through, how much I was putting them through. The instant my brothers came in the room this shifted. Suddenly, we were all there for each other, all of us in the same room, all of us crying and laughing. Within a heartbeat, we knew this was something we were going to share, that we could depend on each other for the support and care we were going to need over the coming days. And the weeks and months and years.

Depending on your family is, to some extent, in your DNA. Depending on strangers is another matter. While my family have drawn on the kindness of friends, extended family and strangers to help get me through, they remain independent people who prefer not to rely on others. I'm the only one who is dependent on others for most of my needs.

I struggled at first. What seventeen-year-old – anyone-of-any-years-old – wants to rely on machines and tubes to breathe, to be kept hydrated? To depend on people to turn you over so your body doesn't become infected with bedsores? What twenty-eight-year-old wants to be fed every meal?

It's been a long process. From the outset, I've had to stare my helplessness in the face. There have been times when I've struggled to overcome denial and alarm. I remember waking up one morning in a terrible panic as it hit me: what if there's a fire? Someone will have to risk their life for mine, because if they don't get me out of here, I'll burn to death. That means someone will have to put my life ahead of theirs. Whatever needs they might have, mine will always trump theirs.

Not having purchase in your own life is tough. You are no longer an independent being, you are back where you started. You have become other people's property. I can only describe it as a gigantic loss. It's as if all the power I'd once had – all the strength and life, the very core of me – leaked out into the sea, leaving me with no strength to resist, no voice, no presence in myself.

At first, in the hospital, being kept alive by machines, cared for by doctors and nurses, I couldn't see my situation for what it was, what it would become. I was ill, my body was broken (maybe just for now), so being looked after seemed a natural part of being in a hospital. If I hadn't needed the care, I wouldn't be there. In this way I resigned myself to being helped, telling myself it wouldn't be like this forever. So, while I wasn't exactly hostile to the help, I was very much in denial – and not always the sunniest of people to be caring for.

Many people ask me – or want to ask me – how I have come to terms with my dependency. To be honest, even ten years on from my accident, I don't quite have the answer. But I think the key thing is that I can now look beyond it. In fact, days can go by when I don't even notice it. My day is my day, my routines are my routines. In the scheme of things, you probably don't think much about cleaning your teeth or washing your hair. Neither do I – and the fact that mine are washed for me doesn't come into it, most days. I've long since realised that I must have help if I'm to go on living my life. Once I'd conceded that dependence was essential, I gave up fighting it. My energy was better spent on other things.

As soon as you can, start depending on yourself as much as you are able. Sure, you may need medical, physical or psychological interventions, but if you begin to build up a self-reliance in whatever capacity you can, this will give you back dignity. Think about where you might regain some element of control, and focus on developing the power to be included and involved in decisions going forward.

Much will depend on the nature of your circum-stances – I couldn't just decide I was going to walk again; you can't suddenly decide you haven't got cancer or another serious condition. But while I still depend on others for physical help, I am now entirely self-reliant when it comes to making decisions about how I lead my life.

There are always new challenges, new circumstances to negotiate. Sometimes I'm shocked all over again by my dependency. Even now, I can't quite take in that this will last the rest of my life. (And, in case you want to ask, my life expectancy is shorter than normal.)

And yet. While there is no getting away from my physical dependence on others, I have my independence too. I don't depend on anyone to think for me. I don't depend on them to talk for me or express opinions for me. I don't depend on them to make decisions for me. I don't depend on them to be creative, to be tenacious, to make choices, or to be a friend to someone. Above all, I don't depend on them to determine who I am at my core. I don't depend on them to *be* me.

This took a while to sink in, but once it did, I was able to put my dependence on others to one side. Instead, I focused on all the things I can still depend on myself to do. Sometimes I think I am now a better version of me. The things I've experienced and learned since my accident have given me the opportunity to be a more thoughtful, more sensitive person than I might otherwise have been.

So, while I can't wash my own hair or make my own meals, in a typical day there are many things I *can* do. By far the most important is that I can determine how I am going to approach each day. It's down to me to decide what I will do between waking up and going to sleep.

It's not that I need every moment timetabled – some days, I just like to chill, watch TV or read – but, like anyone who works from home, I need structure and purpose. I also enjoy setting myself new challenges – like learning Spanish. Each day I set myself a certain number of words to learn or review. While *todavia no soy muy fluido, pero estoy disfrutando el desafio.*

My parents have always worked extremely hard. My entire family has a good work ethic. When I started earning actual money, then an actual living from my speaking engagements and painting, it was a truly empowering feeling. Living with a disability is expensive – paying for extra heating in the winter, air conditioning in the summer, having to always travel with a companion . . . At twenty-eight, still living at home as I write this, it feels good that I can contribute by paying my own bills. Money isn't everything, though. If your change in circumstance prevents you from earning your keep, there are other ways you can contribute to your own family and to society at large.

Independence of spirit, independence of mind – these things mean everything to me. Before my accident, I wasn't terribly engaged in politics or the challenging issues that define us and our place in society. It wasn't that I had no interest, more that I didn't have the confidence to express my opinions. With all I have gone through, I'm acutely aware none of us know what's round the corner, so it's important to snap into action – to think and act and do and effect change while we can. A transformation in your circumstances – for better or worse – can be a wake-up call. For me, it has meant standing up for disability rights, supporting campaigns against poverty and injustice, using the public platform I have been gifted to try to effect change.

Inevitably, this has opened my eyes to the political landscape out there. In my experience, nothing exists in a vacuum. Public spending and the allocation of resources, the way certain groups within the community are portrayed and provided for – ultimately, it all comes down to economic, social and political choices. I have become a lot more opinionated and passionate in my advocacy. Sometimes I can, as my brothers like to say, 'go off on one', but that's fine. There's nothing I like more than winning a noisy debate about something I'm sure I'm right about.

I've also come to see how linked everything is. A more environmentally friendly world would directly contribute to the accessibility and visibility of the disabled community. Fair and adequate benefits for people living with disabilities would enable more of us to actively contribute to society. It's therefore my aim to be an active participant in the debate on disability rights and climate change. Speaking out for people who maybe don't have the confidence to do it themselves or encouraging them to give voice to their opinions has become very important to me. I want to help people express their views, needs or experiences, whether it be on social media or in letters to their MPs, or in contributing to campaigns. Pursuing these goals keeps my mind active and hopefully independent. Some days, this can take a lot of my time.

Taking an interest in the world around me – not just in terms of issues but the individuals I come in contact with – also keeps me feeling independent. After the publication of *The Little Big Things*, I received hundreds of emails and letters from people who were dealing with changes or challenges in their own lives. It was astonishing to me that my experience had touched so many people, and I vowed to reply to as many as I could. I wanted to help them see that, whatever they were facing, there were ways of coping with it and overcoming it.

Knowing my story somehow made a difference, that I had the experience and insight to offer practical advice or emotional support, made me feel incredibly privileged. I have seen so much kindness and goodness in people since my accident, and I've tried to give back as much as I can by actively being there for others. It would be all too easy to see myself as the only worthy recipient of compassion – no one else in my family or friendship group is a *tetraplegic* – but that would be deeply short-sighted. We all of us have challenges, disappointments, needs. We all need bearing in mind. We all need kindness, whatever our circumstances.

Equally, we should all show kindness. Sure, when I was recovering from my accident, my needs might have been so overwhelming that I was unable to care about or for others. But as I became stronger, able to see outside the confines of myself and my litany of needs, it felt good to be able to give back some of that goodness I'd been shown.

Now, I very much enjoy that part of my life. Being aware of the needs of others, being there for my friends and family, being a good friend, being good at being a good friend, is hugely rewarding. This deeper level of friendship has enriched my life considerably. It's not that I am suddenly nosing my way into everyone's lives. It's not as if every time I talk to my friends it's about problems or challenges. For me, it's about making time, listening carefully, thinking about my friends and letting them know that I am there for them. I may not be able to walk but I can listen, and my friendships are an important part of my independence.

There are many different ways in which we can be there for our family and friends. Not everyone shares my love of talking things through. When I was recovering, I saw first-hand how gestures of thoughtfulness can come in all shapes and sizes. Friends, neighbours, and even people who weren't our friends, were keen to show that they were thinking of my family by dropping off food or sending a card. I'll sometimes paint a picture as a thank you or a thinking-of-you, or give careful thought to how I express myself when writing to people who may be frightened by the changes they are facing.

It's funny how physical dependence can be equated with (non-)independence of mind. I've been in situations where someone has asked me a question and then turned from me in the expectation that my mum or my carer will answer it for me. Or where I've not even been addressed. Looking directly at me, they'll ask my carer, 'Oh, what happened to him then?' When I answer for myself, it triggers a flash of surprise. I've also seen how, after talking to me, they've been forced into a recalibration of their initial assumption, and hopefully a lasting one.

Being clear in what I am asking of the people around me is one of the things that I strive hard to do. This allows me to take control of my needs, to communicate them myself rather than waiting for someone to assume they know what I want. In the immediate aftermath of my accident, I relied on my family to communicate for me, but as I found my voice I vowed to keep it. It took time to reclaim the driving seat. In the early days it was a struggle to find the right words to make my complex needs and wishes clear to carers. As my needs have remained consistent over the years, I'm now pretty good at it. I know that it will make our lives – and their job – much smoother. It's OK to take time to find out how best to communicate with those helping you. It's especially difficult to do so during transition periods, when you're feeling your way and nothing is certain. But once you reach that point of clarity . . . Trust me: the dependency you've been feeling will shift.

I want to live the best independent life that I can. I hope this answer has shown that, although I am dependent on others for my physical needs, I am pretty independent when it comes to making choices about how I live my life. I would go as far as to say that, because my mind is continually focused on the things I *can* do and *do* do, it has become sharper and more active. What I feel now is a long way from any sort of dependence.

3

How do you deal with people staring or asking intrusive questions?

THIS IS A question I'm often asked, and it's one I particularly like answering because it shows that others are aware that being disabled brings challenges. It also hints at an empathy. The questioner intuitively understands that, because I'm in a wheelchair and therefore appear different to the vast majority of people, I may be on the receiving end of unwanted attention. It acknowledges that I am different and questions why this needs be scrutinised. It is a sensitive, thoughtful question, and I always try to give a thoughtful response.

The question also shows a desire to know what it's like to be in my situation, to understand how I might be experiencing disability. This opens the door to a significant conversation, because if there's one thing I've learned about becoming 'different', it is the importance of understanding what this difference entails. It gives me the chance to let people know that a life-changing disability is not as scary as someone able-bodied might think. There is great light at the end of the most difficult of tunnels, and we all have the power within us to face or even embrace changes in circumstances and the differences that may arise.

In my post-accident life of difference, I've discovered that I'm not the only one with a story. Since my accident opened my eyes and ears, my life has been enriched by a whole host of people whose lives are different to mine, and no doubt different to yours too. Listening, opening my mind, appreciating their stories, asking questions has been one of the best things that's happened to me. There are people with all sorts of disabilities or challenging circumstances whose lives are so enlightening, so full of strength and hope, that if you listen carefully, any 'difference' soon becomes invisible. Overcoming adversity, no matter how big or small, unites us. Truly listening to the experiences of others is, in my opinion, one of the greatest gifts you can give to yourself. As Leonardo da Vinci once wrote: 'The noblest pleasure is the joy of understanding.'

Don't worry, I realise I've not yet answered the question, so far it's all preamble. Despite what you might be thinking, I do like to answer succinctly. It's only when I feel passionately about something that I allow myself a few words before getting down to addressing the question in hand, which I shall do now.

To be honest, I don't get many people staring at me. I think that's because I sit in a 'normal' wheel-chair, without electronic functions or even a headrest or armrests. It's one of the things I'm particularly proud of because, when I was recovering in Stoke Mandeville, I was told that no one with my level of injury had ever managed permanently in a chair without arm rests and a head rest. It's not that I am anti these wheelchairs – they are brilliant; in the past ten years the technology has improved, making everyday life so much easier for people with limited movement. It's just that, when I was shown the range of wheelchairs on offer, I made the decision to take a more challenging route. I figured that if I didn't try then, I might never. Having been in the hospital for so long at that point, I was feeling defiant. I needed to show I could go beyond expectations. The only concession I would agree to was that the back of my chair would be slightly higher than most conventional wheelchairs, to help me maintain my balance. I have to work very hard on my physical strength in order to keep sitting in my chair, which is why I take my physio very seriously.

Making that decision early on was hugely empowering – albeit challenging for those around me, but I don't regret it for one millisecond. I wasn't exactly known for taking the difficult option before my accident, so came as a surprise to discover that when I was faced with options post-accident, I was able to summon up the power in me – power that might previously have been buried too deep to be of much use – to make some pretty out-there choices. Whatever situation you or your loved ones find yourself in, I'd strongly encourage you to have the courage of your convictions, to trust your instinct and fly in the face of convention. Stubbornness, plus a bit of grit and rebellion, rules.

✳

GOING BACK TO how I cope with people staring at me, it might also be that people don't stare too much because I'm not attached to breathing apparatus and don't have any visible disabilities other than my immobility. When I'm at home I have my hands placed on cushions on my lap, but when I'm out, my hands rest on my lap. So people may not register that I'm a tetraplegic; they might even assume I'm in a wheelchair temporarily.

Then again, it could just be that I don't notice people staring at me. When you're sitting in a wheelchair, you aren't at most people's eye level. For all I know, everyone does stare at me, but I'm not at the right height to see.

I do get asked questions by strangers, but I've never seen them as intrusive. That's probably because I've chosen to be 'out there', talking about being disabled. What's funny is *how* people ask me things. Some just come straight out with it: 'What happened to you, then?' Or, 'Why are you in a wheelchair?' 'Oh, will you ever walk again?' Others skirt around the obvious, as if summoning up the courage to ask what the less inhibited come straight out with. That's OK. Some people are naturally shy or embarrassed. They may even feel that, having asked me to open up, they will have to share something about themselves in return.

I've come to realise that some people are actually afraid of me, as if my disability is contagious and if they come too close it might happen to them. Mad. The scared ones tend to look once, look away, then give me a wide berth, reluctant to register too much about me. There's not much I can do about it – it's not as though I can run after them. But it's made me think how that might have been me, pre-accident, and how limiting that sort of attitude is. If I can change this in just one person every so often, I can feel better about how I might have once behaved.

Children tend to stare the most, possibly because they're at eye level. I've heard many funny comments in my time, along the theme of 'Why is that big man in a buggy?' or, 'Look at that sitting-down man, Mummy, is he too lazy or too tired to walk?' I never mind, especially if their parent brings them over to chat or explains to them that I can't walk and need help getting about. If a child is upset or maybe even frightened, I can reassure them that I am totally fine being in my wheelchair. Once they know that, apart from not being able to move my arms and legs, I'm just like everyone else, children are so accepting. They're also super-inquisitive – I've enjoyed some of my best chats in primary schools or sports clubs. Their questions keep me on my toes.

As a straight talker myself, I prefer the more direct line of questioning. Ask me whatever you want – I'll answer as straightforwardly as possible. I can't hide the fact I'm in this wheelchair. Besides, it's such a part of me now, I can't remember what it feels like not to be in the chair.

Over the past few years, I've noticed that I get asked fewer questions now that everyone is focused on their phones. That can be good and bad. Maybe it's because I'm not that interesting, or perhaps they satisfy their curiosity by googling 'person in a wheelchair, why?' Sometimes I like being ignored like everyone. But I miss those unexpected moments of connection with strangers that leave me laughing, or make me feel seen when I'm feeling invisible. These interactions remind me to get out of my head and to engage with the world. Every time I do this, I feel that the world opens up a little more. You may find the same, if you make the effort to speak to strangers, to make connections that leave you feeling a part of something bigger than yourself.

That's not to say I always need or want people to ask me questions *about* my disability. Sure, at the end of a talk in which I am inviting questions about it, that's great. I'd be gutted if, after I'd spoken for half an hour on my experience, the questions were about Brexit or *Love Island*. But when I'm out shopping or in a club or doing everyday things, I don't want to be defined by my disability. I can chat about many things – politics or the rugby or who should win *Love Island* – and we may have different opinions on those matters, but that has nothing to do with the fact I can't move my legs and arms. In other words, I'm just like you, so we can enjoy conversations that don't touch on my disability.

Having said that, as someone who is 'different' I'd rather be asked about my 'differences' than to have them ignored. Soon after my accident, I had to come to terms with being different to the way I had been before running into the sea. I'd lived seventeen years one way and now I was going to have to live the rest of my life another. The shock of realising this will never go away. It will always be with me in some way. If you have experienced a great change in your life, you will know how seismic it can be, with the effects rippling out endlessly from that one life-changing event. In my case, it was not only because of the harsh change in my circumstances, but because I was forever going to be different from the vast majority of society.

I wasn't a particularly confident person. I preferred being part of the crowd, avoiding anything that would make me stand out – unless it was my prowess on the rugby pitch, or some achievement that distinguished me from my brothers in my parents' eyes. So it was hard to come to terms with this great big physical difference that made it impossible to blend in. This was something I couldn't keep hidden from myself, much less anyone who happened to set eyes on me.

I soon came to see that, while a physical disability needs major physical readjustment (not to mention psychological) it does not wipe out who you are at your core. Besides, we are *all* different at some level. The important thing is how you accept or present that difference. Though it took me some time to adjust, I was able to turn my disability into something positive, accept it, work it and even embrace it.

I believe that we need to respect our similarities and our differences, to resist making judgements before learning why someone is different. As they say, knowledge is power. If we take time to ask questions, listen to the answers, to aim for empathy and understanding, then our lives will be enriched. This is one of the fundamental reasons I'm happy to speak in public, to engage with people on social media and to answer questions about what it is like to live with a disability. If I can break down barriers – even if it means being stared at or asked an intrusive question – then I can go to sleep knowing I've contributed to bridging a few gaps in understanding. For me, it is the connections we make despite, or even because of, our differences that make our world so rich and rewarding.

※

THIS LEADS ME to another question I am often asked – and am always pleased to answer: what assumptions shouldn't you make about disabled people?

While I can't speak for all disabled people – the assumption that we're all the same is the one I hate most – I'll share three that make me uncomfortable.

First: the assumption that I need help. It's very kind of you to be concerned for my welfare, but I'd prefer it if you asked whether I *need* or would like help. I've had people come up and push me when I haven't asked to be moved or have anywhere I need to go. Imagine approaching an able-bodied person and just picking them up and putting them on the other side of the room – it's the same thing. I don't always need to get somewhere.

Second: the assumption that I must be sad or depressed. There seems to be a perception that being disabled is a terrible state to be in, therefore I should be regarded as an object of pity. Sure, sometimes – presumably just like you, disabled or able-bodied – I may feel off, or irritable or I'm having a bad day. But this is rarely to do with being a tetraplegic. It's most probably due to my iPad not working, or my painting not going the way I envisaged, or I'm disappointed that a friend has cancelled our get-together. I can be at odds with the world for many reasons that don't involve being in a wheelchair.

The third assumption I find hard is the one that rules out the possibility that I – or any other person living with illness or disability – can make a positive contribution to society. This infuriates me so much so that I now use my social media presence to high-light the abilities and contributions of disabled people. For decades, the disabled community has been demonised as taking from society without giving any-thing back. This view is myopic and reductive, in my opinion – which is based on research and talking to other disabled people. The truth of the matter is this:

many disabled people have been forced into a situation where they've had to take from the state because they simply can't afford to live, work or function without the equipment or help that they need. If we, as a society, gave disabled people the support they needed in order to live their lives to the best of their abilities, they could give so much to the world. But years of austerity and cutbacks, years of treating the disabled as though they are unable to contribute to society, have created obstacles that hold disabled people back.

The media tends to reinforce the myth that disabled people don't do anything, which doesn't help. Many of the people I talk to have never actually met or spoken to anyone who is disabled, so they're inclined to believe what they read. I guess one of the things that I try to do, is to show that disabled people *can* do things. That we can work, that we can contribute, that we can be fully functioning members of our communities.

What's more, we can contribute positively. Some of you may remember Lauren, from my last book. She and Agnes were on the rehab ward with me in

Stoke Mandeville, so we did a lot of our recovering together. Lauren and I were very much in tune when it came to pushing ourselves in the gym and with our physio. Lauren went from not even knowing about the existence of wheelchair athletes before her accident, to becoming the number one professional wheelchair tennis player in Great Britain. Ten years on, despite further injury and a recent diagnosis of Crohn's disease, she is training hard and hopes to be a part of Team GB in the 2020 games in Tokyo. Her contribution to raising the profile of disabled athletes has been brilliant. Whenever I hear her name I feel this surge of gratitude as I remember being back in that rehab gym, where her positive attitude and determination helped me focus on getting as fit as I could.

Sport is one of those arenas in which people living with disabilities do get some traction and recognition, especially after the Paralympics. I love experiencing that huge support for our athletes who compete with all sorts of disabilities. It's a wonderful feeling to see disabled presenters on TV, to soak up the genuine admiration and respect for what disabled people have achieved. When the media presents the moving stories of how the athletes have overcome adversity and pushed themselves to their limits in order to represent Great Britain, the entire nation is touched by their stories.

Much as I welcome the buzz that lasts for a few weeks around the incredible feats of the Paralympics, I'd prefer all that positivity and recognition to be channelled into the countless disabled people living ordinary lives. Of course our champions should be recognised for what they achieve, but just because you don't represent your country or win medals does not mean you aren't making a positive contribution to society.

Beyond demystifying what it's like to live with a disability, and ridding the world of the misconception that disabled people can't and don't contribute, I believe we need to tear down the barriers that prevent disabled people being fully integrated members of society. We need to look at making venues accessible, making transport accessible. These things stop people from living a normal life. If I can be a voice in getting these issues addressed, then bring it on.

When I feel frustrated about the assumptions made about disabled people, I've learned that the best cure is action. Frustration comes from feeling powerless, and you don't have to be in a wheelchair to feel that way. Speaking out about the barriers that prevent disabled people living full, vibrant lives is incredibly important to me. I have a voice and I'm determined to use it in the service of improving life for others as well as myself. Sure, I can fix a ramp in my own home, but it is much more fulfilling to influence legislation that will improve the lives of tens of thousands.

Like many people who become the 'voice' of a cause, I didn't set out to do this, and I certainly didn't choose it. But engaging in this work has given my life a whole new meaning. When you find life frustrating, I urge you to look for the ways in which you can make a difference. There is always a way, even if it's not obvious immediately.

And next time you come across someone who may be different to you, take a moment before making an assumption. Open your mind to anyone you perceive as 'different'. Instead of assuming you know their story, instead of fearing that difference, why not simply ask them a question instead?

4

Are you in pain?

CONSIDERING THE GRAVITY of my injury, I have suffered remarkably little pain. As my head hit the seabed, I remember a sort of juddering sensation. But displacing four vertebrae in my neck and crushing my spinal cord didn't, as it turned out, actually *hurt*. It was the absence of pain, or any sensation at all, that was the most alarming thing immediately after my accident. I was cold and I was scared, but I didn't *feel* anything. When the paramedics arrived on the beach and put my head in a neck brace and my body on stretcher, I felt no pain. Even when we arrived at the hospital and my trolley crashed through the emergency doors at top speed as they wheeled me straight to X-ray with doctors and nurses running along by my side, like they do in those TV soaps, I felt nothing. When people ask 'are you in pain', it's because they imagine that would be the worst part of an injury like mine. But the absence of pain can be a terrifying thing.

The only true agony I experienced came shortly after those first X-rays, which showed how much my neck had been dislocated. Within a matter of seconds, with more and more people in the room shouting incomprehensible instructions at each other in what sounded like great panic, I was being put in traction. I felt cold cream being smeared on the sides of my head just above my ears and then this tremendous force at either side of my head as two doctors screwed into the bone in order to hook me into a large metal brace that spread over my head like a halo. Then I was clamped on to a pulley that had weights attached to it. This was in the hope that my fourth vertebra, the one that was completely out of alignment, might slip back into place.

This was the pain that made up for the other pain that I couldn't feel. It is hard to describe the sensation as I think my body had gone into shock, but it felt as if someone was drilling into my brain and the pressure of the screws being inserted was almost too much to bear. But after that, apart from a few times, pain didn't come in to it. Discomfort did, though. Soon discomfort became the new pain. Discomfort and bewilderment. Like when the fevers raged through me in the first few days in the hospital in Lisbon, but I was feeling so cold that my teeth would be chattering like a cartoon character. Then suddenly the nurses would come rushing into the room with buckets of ice that they practically threw all over me to get my temperature *down*. It was surreal. Eventually the fevers and infections were reduced but, even now, when my teeth start chattering I know it's a sign that something isn't quite right, that I may have a urinary tract infection or something is inflamed that I can't feel. I'm always comforted by the efficiency of my body. Even though it isn't firing on all cylinders, it can still warn me of invading bacteria, and because I am so used to it now, I can act immediately. Listening to what your body is telling you is crucial in any sort of recovery. I have learned to respect, listen to and obey what mine is signalling to me.

There was no doubt that, even if I felt no pain, my body had suffered great trauma. When traction failed to do the trick, I had to endure a seven-hour operation during which my surgeon opened the front of my neck in an attempt to align my vertebrae. This didn't work, which was devastating enough in itself. Add to that the stress of coming round to find I couldn't speak because there were tubes up my nose and down my throat, then being told I had contracted MRSA and pneumonia . . . The shock sent my body into panic mode, causing my heart rate to drop so dramatically that it flatlined on the machine. And this happened several times, so I had to have a pacemaker fitted.

While I felt no pain, I did imagine pain. I would get this throbbing in my head, which wasn't a head-ache. I would express this as 'something's hurting. I don't know what.' It was frustrating and confusing but the doctors explained this was neuropathic pain, which is very common in patients who've suffered 'catastrophic injury'. The body is in such trauma that it still thinks it's feeling certain things. Because of all my rugby training and time in the gym, I was very aware of the way my body worked. That made it even more scary to find myself unable to navigate the map of my body. It was a whole new learning curve for me to get to grips with.

The neuropathic pain disappeared after a while. I guess as my body readjusted and got used to its new state of being. Now, I get something called autonomic dysreflexia, which is my body's way of telling me that there is pain or an infection or something wrong, somewhere I can't feel it. As with my chattering teeth, I know my body is telling me this because I experience a kind of pins-and-needles sensation in my head. I'm lucky as this is relatively mild, no more than an unpleasant sensation. Some people with a similar level of injury get a throbbing headache or go red in the face. If I ignore mine – which I don't (partly because it happens very rarely) – I can go quite red too. As soon as I'm aware of the first signs, I will call my carer and we go through a checklist of possible causes to see what's occurring. It can be something as simple as a blocked catheter or it can be a sign of infection, which can often be sorted quickly or treated with medication. Then the symptoms disappear.

It's strange how naturally you can feel so much a part of your body, not giving much, if any, thought to how it works. Then something comes along – an accident, cancer, a faulty heart – and all that changes. As soon as I was stable enough, I was transferred from the Lisbon hospital to Stoke Mandeville. I spent the next six months learning to breathe, swallow and eat as if, at the age of seventeen, I had never breathed, swallowed or eaten before. This rehabilitation was both completely necessary and, when I looked at it from the outside in, completely mad. I can only describe these processes as brutal. They involved a myriad of tubes running into various parts of my body, a lot of machinery, plus a great deal of prodding and poking. While I rarely felt pain in the pure sense of the word, I was all too familiar with being uncomfortable.

Take when Scott, my physio, had to teach my muscles to remember how to cough. First he would hook me up to a cough assist machine, via a mask that went over my mouth. Then he would climb onto my bed, straddle me and place his fists under my ribcage as the machine pumped air into my lungs. Taking a breath in, I had to cough it out while he timed it and pushed right up under my ribcage into my diaphragm. This process was hard on my collar bones, and the pressure on my neck was so painful that the only thing I could do was to summon every last bit of power I had in my mind and body to get through it. Afterwards, I'd immediately fall asleep to block out the pain. It's amazing actually how courageous and strong we can be at times of great stress – maybe it's down to a primordial instinct to survive. I knew I had to be able to cough, swallow and breathe without assistance if I was to have any chance of getting to the next stage of my recovery. The goal can make the difficulty tolerable.

Later, when I was spending less time hooked up to the ventilator and more of the day on an oxygen tank, I was downstairs in the café one day with some of my school mates and brothers when I began to feel dizzy and confused with a weird sort of head pain. Tom rushed me back upstairs – my brothers loved whizzing me around the place – and after the nurse went through her checks, it turned out the nurse on duty before her had forgotten to switch on the tank. My oxygen tank had actually been giving me no oxygen, so it was no wonder I had experienced this awful sensation. Tom got me back just in time; for once, I was grateful for the Formula One wheelchair-manoeuvring skills that my brothers competed over.

It wasn't only the physical sensation of discomfort that troubled me during my recovery. I also felt tremendously *invaded*, and that became a source of emotional and psychological pain. On top of the trauma it had suffered, my body was no longer my own. This was an indignity that it – I – often wanted to rebel against. I would panic, too, in those early days. While panic doesn't hurt as such, shock and terror would jolt through me with such intensity it was like a physical manifestation of pain.

In Portugal I'd grown used to being raised up in bed, but on arrival at Stoke Mandeville the doctors were adamant that I had to lie completely flat in case I damaged my neck further. The worst thing about this was having to be tilted every few hours to relieve the pressure on my skin. I was strapped to the bed and as it tilted my body would lean ever so slightly one way. To me, that lean felt huge. Every time I was tilted I flew into panic, convinced I was going to fall off. This soon became unsustainable; after a few days, the doctors agreed I could transfer to a bed that allowed me to sit up, the same type of bed I sleep in to this day. But I was so terrified about being transferred from one bed to another, I had to be given drugs to calm me down. Trust me, that level of panic is a weird sort of pain.

As you can probably tell, much of that pain was psychological rather than physical. I don't want to be over-dramatic and say it *hurt*, but it did cause me mental angst. Coping with that was something I think of as part of my recovery. And that word – recovery – is the key in answering this question, because once I felt able to engage in my own recovery, once I grasped how best I could achieve that, I began to view the pain or discomfort I suffered as a step towards regaining control of my body, myself and my situation. Very little of my recovery was comfortable, but over time it became less uncomfortable. As I began to see results, it seemed almost worth it.

At Stoke Mandeville, I was reliant on others to determine the best course of recovery for me, to go along with their advice and techniques. Broadly, the expertise of the very knowledgeable, caring team there was fantastic. But there were one or two slip-ups which still have consequences for me today. The most troublesome was to do with the wheelchair I was first put in, as it didn't have the correct armrests, so my shoulders weren't supported properly. Of course, the muscles around my shoulders were non-existent as a result of the accident, so it was just down to the ligaments and tendons to keep the joints together. Without the muscles, these stretch over time, so if the elbows aren't supported there's a gap in the joint. Now when I do physio or sit awkwardly, it feels as though my shoulder isn't in the joint properly, and this can cause me great discomfort.

Nowadays, because of the lack of movement elsewhere in my body and the pressure up top, when I do physio I get muscle ache in my neck and shoulders – like everyone else. But maybe what I'm better at than some is knowing to stop what I'm doing rather than carry on and make it worse. As with everything in this process, I've become better at not pushing myself to extremes. I know I will pay for it and it's just not worth it. There's always later or tomorrow, so it's pointless putting myself through undue work or stress. Much better to listen to what my body is telling me, even if I can't feel it, and act on it to stop things getting worse. Learning to listen to the signals of your body is essential for all of us, but for some of us it can be life-threatening to ignore the signs.

Any change in your physical or medical circumstances requires patience, and that's especially true when you're exploring the new parameters of your ability. I would advise anyone going through any such adjustments to listen carefully to advice you are given, play around with variations within a limited, acceptable range, then, over time, decide on what suits you best. It's very important not to force yourself to go all out, ignoring the warning signs. You risk causing long-term damage to your body that will put you right back to where you started, or a few steps further back.

It's not just a physical thing either. I have struggled with the loss of dignity. There was a period when I used to get uncomfortably cold when I was out and about, but I'd refuse to have a blanket over my legs. At the time, I hated being seen with a blanket over me – it made me feel – and, as I saw it, look – ill. The resulting chill would inevitably leave my body in a bit of a depleted state, prone to picking up infections, which led to more discomfort and illness. It took a while before I made the link between cause and effect but, once I did, I was able to prioritise my health over the way I thought people saw me. Now, if I need a blanket around me, I get a blanket put on and I stay healthy. The alternative is too high a price to pay for dignity: an infection will put me in bed, being in bed means I can't paint or give talks, or see my friends. There's no point in being stubborn or wilful for the sake of it. Having a blanket around me – which most people won't even register, assuming they notice me at all – is a short cut to a healthier, happier time.

It is strange that people assume your relationship to your body is gone if you are paralysed, when actually you become much more acutely aware of it than ever before. I have learned to have a level of respect for my body and what it is capable of that I don't think I had before the accident, when I took my physicality for granted. It's one of life's ironies that you rarely recognise what you have until it is gone, so after a traumatic event or life-changing diagnosis, it's even more important to understand what you can and can't do, to learn what causes you pain or discomfort, and how best you can reduce it, even if it means making some compromises along the way.

5

What surprised you most after your accident?

A SURPRISE CAN dazzle you with the joy of the unexpected, but it can also crush you with the weight of its unexpectedness. Never being able to walk again, after running into the sea to cool off, was not the kind of surprise I'd ever wanted. But the consequences of my accident have brought about some massive surprises that I guess I'd never have experienced otherwise.

I could fill the rest of this book detailing the things that have surprised me over the past ten years. The gentleness of a stranger lifting a drink to my lips; the wordless communication between my friends when we're on a night out and one of them takes me to empty the urine from my leg bag; the email from someone I've never met who has read my book and wants to share their private story; the lengths my school went to accommodate me when I went back to do my A levels, switching lessons and timetables across the year and honouring my sports scholarship even though I was in a wheelchair; the fundraising that pupils, parents and staff there did for me, which enabled me to buy equipment such as my FES (functional electrical stimulation) bike that has made such an impact on my recovery; the car our friend converted from a manual to an automatic for us, to make driving me around easier for my family and carers; the encouraging whoops and whistles from a group of female prisoners as I gave my talk; the joy of being out in the sun; the comfort of routine.

The list is endless but, drilling down, there are three things that stand out: the kindness of friends, family and strangers; the gratitude I've experienced about a whole host of things I previously took for granted; and the unexpected joy of incremental progress.

It was kindness that lifted me up and carried me through the darkest and most difficult of times. It arrived immediately – from the two guys who slid me, with such gentleness and not a hint of panic, onto a bodyboard as my friends ran for help; the paramedic who held my hand in the air ambulance from the beach to the hospital in Lisbon; the locals who stayed with my friends and helped them track down where I'd been sent. The kindness continued on and on, from the medical team in the hospital in Lisbon to the nurses in Stoke Mandeville who, once I was well enough, allowed my friends to visit at all hours, turning a blind eye to the time; and the number of those friends who made the long trek from Dulwich and the slightly shorter trek from Berkhamsted to Stoke Mandeville several times a week. The kindness in this paragraph alone could have sustained me for much of my lifetime.

I was kept afloat by kindness and it came from everywhere, in all forms. Ten years on, I still have the ginormous pink card with the words 'To My Girlfriend' crossed out and replaced with 'To My Boyfriend', that my friend Harry thought it hilarious to send me. Inside this one huge card are all of the cards, letters and drawings that I received while in hospital – from my friends; from my parents' and brothers' friends; from family near and far; from past and present teachers, rugby coaches and team mates; pupils at my primary and secondary schools; people from our village that I either knew or didn't know, to friends of friends who none of us knew.

For some time, while I was ill with infections and fevers and largely out of it, I wasn't even aware that all these cards were arriving. But my parents and brothers put every one of them up on all the available surfaces around my bed. I will never forget waking up one morning, more alert to my surroundings, and seeing all those cards in their glorious colours, shapes and sizes, glowing at me from across my bed. I had this literal jolt of surprise that, when I think back, still reverberates down the years. It was as if I'd been dreaming in black and white, then awoke to this Technicolor world – an array of colours and images enveloping me with their love. As soon as Mum arrived, I asked her to bring them to me one by one. I spent the next few days so absorbed in reading them that, for the first time in my life, words became everything. From the long, emotional identification of shock or disbelief, to the short 'thinking of you' and everything in between, each one of those messages was a source of comfort and inspiration to me. I would read them over and over again, taking new things from them every time.

The expressions of love, the kindness that zinged off the pages, found their way into me. Ten years on, I can open the big pink card, pull out any one of the smaller cards and rattle off from memory what's written inside. The cards from my time in hospital have played a big part in my personal history, forming a sort of written and visual narrative that helps me piece this period together, especially the parts that I struggle to remember.

Sending a card or a message to those who are suffering or going through something life-changing – good or not so good – is just about one of the kindest acts possible. It still makes me emotional that people were bearing me in mind, let alone putting pen to paper. It may feel to you that it is a small gesture, but to the recipient it could be everything.

You don't need to send an essay or stress over what is or isn't appropriate to say, though of course sensitivity is key. In my case, most of the messages I received came in the first few weeks, when people steered clear of the fact I was unlikely to ever walk again. Looking back, I'm grateful for that.

It's knowing you're in someone's thoughts that counts. However grim the situation, believe me, someone who's been through a life-changing trauma will want to hear from you. If it's hard for you, imagine how hard it is for them. Reaching out will, I promise you, make a difference to their day. And don't wait too long. Those initial messages are life-saving. Texts, WhatsApps, emails – you don't even need to hand-write a message of support. I received plenty of messages by text and email. When I couldn't access my phone, my brothers kept and read to me every electronic message. Those messages meant just as much to me as the cards.

There were other acts of kindness that sprung up around us. The unobtrusive procession of friends and family who would leave meals on the doorstep of our house, so that my mum didn't have to think about cooking when she came home from a long day at the hospital. My family never ate so well. Imagine my surprise when the dads from our annual local fathers-and-sons camping trip came to the hospital to see me one evening and Steve, who was renowned for cooking awesome fry-ups, produced a plate of freshly made eggs, bacon, mushrooms, hash browns and beans, just for me. It meant *so* much. I still remember how delicious it tasted. Even now, on the rare occa-sions when I have a fry-up, I think of his kindness.

It's natural that we want to be there for our loved ones in times of crisis, but it's often not possible to be physically present. I wasn't up to having visitors beyond my immediate family and closest friends for a while. Our friends and extended family, shocked and upset by what had happened to me, desperately wanted to support us as a family, to be with us in our moment of need and crisis, but they couldn't. Instead of standing by feeling useless, they deployed their skills in ways they knew would help us – arranging the food, looking after my younger brother Dom who had to go back to school, and too many other favours to list here. If you feel powerless or excluded from front-line care, ask yourself what you can do in practical terms to make life better for those you are wanting to help. There are many ways to show you care; giving a little time to thinking of things that may not be immediately obvious can be invaluable.

My mum was shored up by the messages her friends sent her every day, checking how she was, whether she needed anything. They made it clear that they were there for her, but understood entirely if they didn't hear back (if you are in the midst of a crisis, you can do without having to satisfy the egos or needs of others). They were on constant standby to do anything, from the smallest of tasks to being with her at the hospital. At first she relied on them for practical help, but later, as I got stronger and the days got longer, Mum's friends would come and spend time with her. I would listen to them chatting; sometimes, as I drifted off for a nap to recover from a tough physio session, the sound of their voices was comforting – not only for the familiarity but the knowledge that Mum had company.

No amount of kindness could take away the pain or difficulty from my situation. The sheer power of collective kindness couldn't make me walk again – though sometimes it felt like it might. But by showing me and my family that they were there for us, they made what could have been an unbearable situation bearable. When we strip away the noise and nonsense of the world around us, in our busy, frantic daily lives, kindness is, I believe, one of humanity's greatest gifts. As trite as it might sound, we all need to show more of it to each other. One small act of kindness can have ripples that spread much further than you might imagine.

And you know what? There's a lot to be said for small gestures of kindness even when there isn't a crisis. Sending someone a gift or a card or a message expressing your admiration or love for them can give them a nice surprise. What's more, kindness leads to kindness. If it weren't for the kindness I was shown, I don't think I would have truly understood what a difference it makes. Now, where possible, I reach out to others in various aspects of my life.

The kindness shown to me surprised me over and over again. To this day, I can be stopped in my tracks when I think about it. The feeling I get when this strikes brings me to the second biggest surprise I've had: discovering the true meaning of gratitude.

It's funny because at the time when the nurses were turning my body every few hours to prevent me from getting bedsores, or the machines were being checked to ensure they were doing their thing, I didn't feel too much gratitude. I felt as if my body was the property of anyone but me, that the machines bleeped too loudly or were demanding my dependence. But now, when I think of the care involved, the dignity I was given, the cheerfulness of the nurses when I was grumpy and unresponsive, the fact that I didn't suffer from bedsores (which would have set my recovery back further), and that the machines literally kept me alive, my gratitude to them feels like a tangible thing that I can see in front of me. Feeling this gratitude is such a mood enhancer that it allows me to see past the trauma of that period to all the positive things that were happening, even if I didn't experience the gratitude in the moment.

My first encounter with the overwhelming force of gratitude happened when I was taken from the intensive care unit to the acute ward. If you haven't seen sunlight for five weeks, then you have to believe me when I say that I was literally mesmerised by the light streaming in through the windows at the far end of my new home, St Andrew ward. Lying in my bed, looking out into the light, fresh air coming in through the open window, was one of the most vividly beautiful experiences of my life. How could I, I thought, have taken all this for granted, even for a nanosecond? So what if I couldn't move, or breathe without a ventilator, or eat without a feeding tube? The purity and joy of light, the sun and the air, were enough to sustain me.

Undoubtedly, this was the over-the-top reaction of someone who had been denied all these things for so long. Naturally, I was still frustrated that I couldn't breathe or eat for myself. But sometimes in life, you are gifted a moment when the splendour of the things you have always taken for granted become crystal clear. Air, sunlight and – later, when I was allowed my first sip – water. I'd never even *thought* about these things. The surprise of suddenly understanding their value *and* being aware of feeling gratitude, is a pretty powerful, intoxicating thing.

Even today, thousands of glasses of water later, I can be drinking and, while it's hard to quite put the feeling into words, feel gratitude for it in that moment. The same for the feeling of the sun on my face. I don't experience this very often, because being too hot isn't good for me, so on the odd occasion when I sit out in the sun and it warms my face, I feel it afresh, and I'm thankful. Being grateful is a part of acceptance. It marks a new understanding; a new appreciation of things you may well have taken for granted. It is in itself a transformative experience. You never go back again.

The gratitude I feel for life continues, though I must admit I don't think about it every day, as I mostly just get on with living, as we all do. But the gratitude I feel towards those who care for me, those who bear me in mind, those who are kind to me, can never be over-estimated. I can't express gratitude out loud for every little thing my carer or my family, friends and strangers do for me – I'd never be saying anything other than thank you – but I can show my appreciation and I can recognise what it is that people do for me.

What do I take away from this? We all, from time to time, need to recognise what we have, to be surprised by it as if for the first time. We must learn to look around at the things we appreciate, however basic, to take a moment to feel grateful and enjoy them. The same goes for the people in our lives – it's so easy to take them for granted. Gaining this new, grateful perspective can reboot us when things may feel a little stuck.

And speaking of things being a little stuck, the final thing that has most surprised me since my accident is my new-found ability to recognise progress. Not to *make* progress – we all know we can do that in some form or other – but to understand what it feels like to quantify it, to measure it, sometimes in a matter of seconds and minutes, and still feel pumped about it.

When you are stripped right back to not being able to do the very basic things that keep you alive – breathe, eat, walk – you can go one of two ways: forwards or backwards. If you have the option to go forwards, then there is a route you need to follow to either make progress or to get back to where you were. I was never going to walk again, I understood that. But there was no physical reason I wouldn't, in time, be able to breathe for myself or be able to eat solid food. It wasn't going to happen overnight though. These were processes that needed to be done slowly and safely, so progress would have to be measured in minutes at a time. The first day I spent breathing for five minutes off the ventilator and on the oxygen tank, I was exhilarated. Five minutes. When had I ever thought of progress in five-minute slots? Or of eating in half-biscuit portions? But every second of those five minutes and every mouthful of my first half-biscuit was hard-fought, hard-won progress. Each step made me feel better; each next step made me feel better still. Even on days when I went backwards, when I was too exhausted to go on for another few seconds, I was able to bank the progress I had been making and look forward to the next day when I could make some more.

In his poem 'The Love Song of Alfred J. Prufrock', T. S. Eliot wrote about measuring his life out in coffee spoons. In making these small amounts of progress, this is exactly what I felt I was doing as I learned to breathe and eat again. It was hard, it was slow; progress was often incredibly arduous. But after seconds, minutes, quarter-hours, half-hours, hours, days, I got there.

Making progress is cumulative, actually and psychologically. You find that if you can make progress in one element of your recovery, you become clearer in your thinking and sense of self. This can have a knock-on effect, empowering you to make progress in other areas. Being able to breathe and eat again made me want to make progress on my strength. Thus began my quest to push myself out of the hospital in my wheelchair. That also required me to walk before I could run, so to speak; just learning to push the wheelchair was made up of hundreds of tiny movements that took months to develop.

It's natural to want to progress in big stages, to jump from one thing to another and 'get there'. So much of what is celebrated in our culture is the triumphant achievement – the headline-grabbing end result, or the 'big win'. But if your life changes course, forcing you to re-evaluate or find new ways of going forward, then there is nothing more empowering than being able to recognise the achievement of incremental progress. Don't get me wrong. This kind of slow progress is tough; it takes enormous reserves of patience and gritted teeth, but it's worth it. Not only in the actual making of the progress but in being able to recognise and value every step of the journey. No step is too small. Every step is huge, however small.

Life is full of surprises. I continue to find myself surprised all the time. Who knew I'd be able to paint using my *mouth*? Who knew I'd be able to address a roomful of strangers and talk about myself? Who knew that the sun on my face could feel quite so renewing? If you open yourself to appreciating the very basic things this world has to offer; if you think about what you might do for others to enhance their lives; if you can recognise the progress you have made on any number of things, however small, then you can surprise yourself over and over again.

6

How did you find acceptance of
your situation?

THIS IS THE question that goes to the core of how I
have lived my life since my accident. Acceptance of
where I am, rather than where I was, is behind
everything I have thought and said and done in the
last ten years. In my opinion, finding acceptance of
whatever life throws at us and those we love best
shows how the power we have in us can help find a
way forward and reshape the way we go on.

Whatever situation you may be facing, I believe

there are some key stages early on in any process of change or adaptation that you need to go through in order to come out the other side. When I look back, there is no doubt in my mind that these stages were the foundations upon which I built my new life. I may not have realised this at the time – I think no one ever does – but when I look at where I am now, and how I have arrived here, I can see the process clearly. The fact is that I can now actually forget from time to time that I'm in a wheelchair. I can look forward to having my shower and cup of tea in the morning, and I can enjoy meals without constantly thinking: I'm being fed this food by someone else. I can look way past my dependence to focus on a more independent-dependence. This, I strongly believe, is down to the stages I went through in accepting what had happened to me.

Realising that things have changed, or shifted in some way, plays a critical part in any process of adjustment or change. While at first you may deny, or simply not realise, that things have changed or are about to change, as a crisis deepens, you can't help but realise the severity of the situation. You become increasingly aware that your life has shifted on its axis and you are heading for somewhere else: uncharted territory.

If you are immediately post-accident or diagnosis, for example, in those first dark days my advice would be to try not to take on more than you can mentally or physically cope with. While I knew immediately after my accident that something potentially catastrophic had happened – how could I not? – something shut me down, preventing me from thinking too hard about the reality of the situation I was in. The state of numbness that I was in offered protection, and I am glad I allowed it, instead of fighting against it. The body is incredibly clever in how it shields us from absorbing an overwhelming experience all at once.

Ideally, you will be protected by others around you while you are in this immediate state of shock. You need to trust that they will find the power in them to do this, however grim things may seem. From the moment I was pulled out of the sea, immobile and freezing, my friends knew something terrible had happened. It is unimaginable to think, as I lay on the beach waiting for the air ambulance, that one of my friends would have leaned over and told me: 'There go your dreams of making the rugby firsts next year, Frase, or any year for that matter.' Similarly, my parents, who were told on arrival at the hospital that my injuries were so severe I would never walk again, were hardly likely to hotfoot it from the doctor's office to break it to me that I was now a tetraplegic. As much as I couldn't have heard it at that point in time, they couldn't have voiced it either. No one close to me, or caring for me, was going to tell me until the right moment.

So, how to explain the actions of the Portuguese nurse, who about ten days into my hospital stay, checking my vitals one morning, told me: 'You know, don't you, that you are never going to move your arms and legs again?'

My immediate thought was: *What?* That's *impossible*, he must have the wrong patient, but I didn't say anything. Fortunately my mum came back into the room and the nurse left. Looking back, when I can allow myself to feel the enormous weight and consequence of those words, I realise that something inside me was able to shut that information down, to bury it deep in some part of my muddled thoughts. I still had enough inner strength, be it self-defence or sheer willpower, to protect myself – and my parents, who for all I knew had not yet been told this – from such a catastrophic diagnosis. As fevered up as I was, I still managed to exercise enough control not to take on more than I could cope with. I appreciate now that this was something that helped me enormously going forward.

I have no idea what could have motivated the nurse to speak so out of turn. Maybe he thought that the sooner I knew, the better. I'm pretty certain it wasn't prompted by unkindness. Perhaps experience had taught the nurse it was better for patients to face facts at the first possible opportunity. Maybe now, ten years down the line, I can appreciate this a bit more. Perhaps he felt this shock would fortify me for what I was going to have to face. I wish I could ask him.

There is no doubt it was too early for me. I needed more time to come to the realisation that something huge had happened to me, to grow from there into knowing what that meant for my future or how grave it all was. I know for sure that you need time to adjust to the realisation itself before you can take on what has happened to you. Even when I surfaced, I managed to filter information, lodge it and come back to it later. You don't need to know everything in this early stage.

If you are fortunate enough to have family or friends around you, or are under the care of a medical team, my advice in the early stages is to surrender the weight of control to the experts. They will have the power in them to see you through the beginning of any major change to your life. You don't need to carry the burden all by yourself. There can be great comfort and relief in embracing the love and support around you. However vulnerable or frightened you are feeling, with the love of others you can face darkness and look through to the other side.

It's also OK to be scared – and it's totally OK to unbottle your emotions and to cry. Understanding this has been so liberating for me, a real eye-opener. I know that my brothers and some of my friends from the holiday feel the same. We were probably a bunch of 'typical blokes' who, before my accident, didn't openly show the more vulnerable side of ourselves. Obviously, the shock of seeing me induced a physical release of tears from just about everyone who came to visit me in the hospital in those early days, but actually it was more than that. Perhaps it was an inbuilt sense of release – one of the very worst things, short of death, had happened to me – but I was still alive, if not quite kicking.

Showing emotion is something I have continued to embrace, even as I got stronger and things became less bewildering. Even now, when things are manageable and normal, I'm not afraid to show my emotions – sad or happy. This is something that has helped me enormously through difficult times. My parents and brothers are the same. You should have heard us – a right cacophony of tears and laughter – when my brother Will and Sian got married.

As you adjust to your situation, the power in you will help you manage fear and uncertainty. It became unsustainable to me to live my life in a state of fright and apprehension. I came to realise that if there was a fire I'd be saved and it didn't actually matter that I couldn't save anyone else (unless they could sit on my lap and be wheeled out with me). Now I have found that acceptance in me, I reckon I can face the same fears and uncertainties as everyone else – the trials and tribulations of daily life, as well as qualms about the future. I need to earn a living, whether I can move my arms and legs or not. The ability to support myself means I can live in far less fear and uncertainty than most, even those who can use their arms and legs.

In those early days, there are things that you can do to help you move to acceptance. Start by taking notice of things going on around you. As I came out of my fog of denial and despair, I became aware that not everyone in my family was able to cope with what had happened to me equally. When I was in intensive care, Will would sit at the end of my bed and stroke my feet. At the time he'd just had an operation on his ankle and his physio had told him to massage his tendons to maximise their flexibility. Will thought if he did this to me, some sort of feeling would come back and I would be able to walk again.

Realisation came slowly to me but when it came, it kind of flooded in. You reach a moment when you can't go back. The situation you are in simply becomes your reality. From that point on, you have embraced it. Once I'd overcome the weight of denial, once I began to actively engage in what had happened to me and what was going on around me, I was in the right mental state to begin accepting what had happened and what I was facing. I was able to accept the situation I was in, which was a whole lot different to the one I'd been in before I'd run into the sea.

There is a thin line between denial and acceptance. While I was no longer denying I'd had a serious accident and that the consequences were grave, I wasn't exactly ready to accept I would never walk again. What I did do was accept that the situation I was in was bad. As I woke up to this, as I slowly began to 'own' it, the going began to get a hell of a lot tougher. It's one thing to lie in your hospital bed, helpless in almost all aspects of being alive, and another to see what you can do about it.

My life was being lived in stages – from the earthquake of the accident to the seismic shift of total dependence on machines and people, then to the more gradual, smaller shifts. In accepting my situation as real, urgent and, most importantly, *mine*, it was now all about moving through each stage with my eyes open to what was happening. It was also about what I could do to affect my well-being and under-standing. Part of that was accepting that I needed help. To admit that some of that help – even the help I wanted to resist – might actually be helping me.

This lesson truly hit home as I was working with my physio, Scott. He was coaching me on breathing and swallowing, so I could come off the ventilator and eat solid food. Later, he showed me how to cap-italise on the movement in my neck and shoulders. All of this was geared to me being less dependent and more actively involved in my own rehabilitation. Because I was so used to exercise and sport, using my body to compete and win, working with Scott made me feel alive again. He made me feel that I was able to do things for myself and make choices. Yes, I was dependent on him, and a host of other things and people, but I could see that if I engaged with him, I could positively impact on my broken state of being and take those first figurative steps on the road to recovery and self-determination. Suddenly it all made sense. I saw what Scott was doing was coaching me in a fight for survival, and I wanted to be as active as possible in this engagement.

It may be that other elements of recovery or taking control appeal more than others. For me it was the physio, for some it may be less physical, more emotional – perhaps therapy or counselling. For others it may be engaging with medication, treatment or rehabilitation. Whatever you are going through, accepting the situation you are in will enable you to take back control.

This much I know: it was when I started to actively engage in my own recovery, be it through Scott, through listening and acting on advice given to me by those caring for me, that my recovery began. It enabled me to see the nurses and doctors not just as functional figures 'doing their job' but as individuals who were invested in helping me recover. Humanising them led to the next development: as I found my voice again, I began to talk to them, to ask questions, to make sense of what was going on around me, what machine was doing what, which doctor or nurse was responsible for different parts of my care. As I engaged with them person to person, they began to see me as more than just a patient. It also enabled me to talk more to my parents about the future. This was when I first floated the idea of me going back to school at some point.

Engaging with those looking after me is something I continue to this day. My carers and I spend so much time together that it's inevitable we chat beyond the confines of my needs. It makes everything much easier – even enjoyable. There is never any pressure on my part for them to engage with me – if they don't feel like it then it's totally fine. I can read their moods as they can read mine. Some mornings, I just don't feel like talking. Nothing to do with being disabled – I'm simply not at my best every morning. What I have learned is that, in this situation, actually in most situations, it's better to communicate, to be open and honest, than to do things begrudgingly.

Acceptance can feel like a fridge-magnet emotion – trite and easy to say. But anyone who has come to terms with a life-changing situation like paralysis, serious illness or grief will tell you that true acceptance is hard work, and can be extremely challenging. What's more, it is an ongoing process – some days are easier than others, even when the immediate crisis has passed and you feel you should be 'over it'. So when I ask you to consider accepting whatever it is that you are going through, please believe that I do so knowing how difficult that journey can be. But acceptance allows us hope, even if it is hope for a very different future to the one we had imagined. It is hard to hope when we are still facing backwards into the past. Accepting the present means allowing hope for the future, and that is what I want for myself and others.

For me, there is one question that I am often asked, the answer to which I think shows that acceptance is a healthy option. The question is this: do you think you will ever walk again? The answer, in a nutshell, is no. But that is not to say that people with a similar disability to me won't ever be able to walk again. There have been some amazing advances in surgery, particularly in stem cell transplantations, science, medicine and technology since my accident, and I am fascinated by many of them. In fact, I am now an ambassador of the UK Stem Cell Foundation and have been working with them to raise awareness of the important research being done in this area.

Basically, a stem cell is a cell that can become another type of cell in the body. Because they can become different types of cells – say skin, muscle or a nerve cell – they offer the potential to treat conditions and illnesses such as blood cancers, Parkinson's, heart disease and, as in my case, spinal cord damage. I became interested in the subject about five years after my accident when I read about Darek Fidyka. After undergoing pioneering surgery in which cells from nerves that ran from his nose to his brain were injected into a tiny gap in his spine, Darek was able to walk again with the help of leg braces and a frame. The transplanted stem cells enabled the damaged nerve cells to regrow, restoring his spinal cord sufficiently that he regained feeling in his legs, bladder and bowels.

In the very early stages, when I was in the hospital in Portugal, my parents read up about the possibilities of repair in spinal cord injuries. I guess, like many of us, they needed some hope to cling on to. 'Imagine what medical science could do in five years' time,' Mum told me. But they never mentioned it again, never even making me engage with this side of their way of coping. For all I know, they sought advice from doctors, or from patients who were in similar situations to me. I expect they did. Being armed with knowledge is an empowering thing. But they respected my wish to get on with my life, to be present in the moment, to use all the power within me to make progress, explore new opportunities and live my life in the way I wanted to. This has been one of the key factors in me enjoying my life post-accident. If I'd had to take on board their 'hopes' that I would walk again, this would have no doubt meant a different path forward.

That isn't to say you can't have hope. You can. In fact I would say that you absolutely must. But for me it's all about where you place that hope, how much of it is realistic. If it's unrealistic, you risk diverting your focus from what might actually, in the here and now, allow you to live your best life. It's unlikely that stem cell transplantation will advance to such an extent in my lifetime that I walk again. What's the point in hoping or thinking that it might? Personally, I'm not holding out. Walking again just isn't on my horizon. So, for me, putting that possibility aside is the best course of action. I genuinely feel that pinning all my hopes on a cure would keep me from accepting my paralysis and living my life as it is. It would be a kind of denial in that I am in the situation I am in. I don't want to wake up every day with a false or unrealistic sense of hope, or to pursue a dream that wouldn't ultimately result in me walking again.

But that doesn't stop me hoping, or working for others in future generations – possibly even children being born today. Working with the Foundation makes me feel alive to the possibility of advances in stem cell transplants. I read as much as I can to stay up to date, as well as take part in fundraising activities so that this important area of research can receive as much funding as possible.

I think what I'm trying to say is that to live is to live your best life. Even if your circumstances change in the way mine have, by accepting them and building on them the best you can, you can still live your best life. Since my accident I have achieved things, done things that I never thought I ever could or would. If I'd spent my time looking way beyond my own life, hoping for a cure, there's no way I would have had the mental energy and focus to paint or speak in public or be a good friend or son, or be true to myself. Live in the moment.

7

How do you handle setbacks?

SEVERELY CRUSHING MY spinal cord as my head hit the seabed on a beautiful summer's afternoon, and never walking or moving my arms again, is possibly as big a setback as they come. When I think about it like that, I guess that everything in my life since that moment has been about accepting and embracing this ultimate setback. So, you could say that this whole book is an answer to this question.

Before my accident, if you'd asked me how I dealt

with setbacks, I'd have answered: not very well. If you take the view that a setback is an impediment, an obstacle, then I just wouldn't have put myself in a situation where I'd have to face one. From as early as I can remember I played it safe. I was frightened of any sort of failure. If I thought I wasn't going to be able to do something, rather than put my mind to it, I'd either find ways to get out of the situation or get so anxious I messed it up anyway.

When I joined Dulwich College in the sixth form – a year before my accident – I was lucky enough to have joined on a sports scholarship. That meant I had to commit myself to two sports a year: training, representing the school and keeping up my team spirit and focus. In reality, while I was just about OK at cricket, I mostly concentrated on rugby, playing in the First XV, which meant a lot of time in the gym in addition to training and matches. I loved the discipline and commitment of the training; most of the time I was good at it. But I didn't always enjoy the matches because of the pressure, a lot of which I put on myself.

I felt I had to always perform in order to earn my scholarship. I couldn't fail. And because I was so frightened of failing, there were times when, injured, even just mildly, I'd get it into my head that the actual physical pain was worse than it was. I'd find a way of getting out of the next match in case I let the team down. Basically, back then, if I had an excuse, a way out, I would use it.

When I look back now, I realise this wasn't a healthy way of thinking or doing things. It caused me to miss out on many opportunities, especially in rugby. I'm not saying I'd have made it as a pro or gone to the top or anything unrealistic, but I know that I could have represented the school and my county more, and been satisfied that I'd given it my all. But my former self was too afraid to confront the possibility of not doing well, or doing something that resulted in a setback for the team. When I faced challenges that required me to do something different from the norm, or something I felt might be uncomfortable, I'd start to doubt myself. Rather than risk failure, I'd avoid the situation entirely. To be honest, I think it became something I'd learned to do and I fell into the pattern too easily.

I can say, with a good deal of confidence, this is no longer the case. At a certain point in my recovery, after I had accepted what had happened to me and faced the fact there was no going back, I realised I had nothing to lose by rising to the challenges that lay ahead. More importantly, it struck me like a thunderbolt that, if I *didn't*, I'd be missing out on living my fullest and most fulfilling life. Also, there was more at stake. Take breathing, for instance. If I hadn't conquered all the difficult, tiring exercises Scott devised for me, I'd have been on the ventilator for longer, possibly forever. As this was something I had the option to change, I had little choice but to put the idea of failure aside, to be as positive about succeeding as I could. Yes, it took a while; yes, it was uncomfortable, often I was bad at it and 'failed', but even the smallest amount of progress soon became a measure of success. As I've mentioned, progress – however small, however slow – is the most important factor in unlocking any sense of the fear of failure. Once you see progress for what it is – a positive step forward – I believe you can achieve more or less anything you set your mind to.

My massive setback allowed me to reboot my entire life. In a situation that could have been overwhelmingly bleak, the clarity with which I re-evaluated my fear of failure has been a bright, life-changing silver lining. Of course, you don't need to experience a setback as catastrophic as mine to reconsider how you face setbacks in your own life. Challenges come in all shapes and sizes and are largely unpredictable, but our reaction to them, the way we deal with the consequences, is always within our control. As soon as I realised this, I entered into uncomfortable situations with a different mindset, telling myself, oh well, I'll just do it, rather than worrying about the potential for failure.

Take speaking in public. Before I returned home after my accident, I'd done everything – and I mean *everything* – I could to get out of speaking out loud in class or anywhere else that involved groups of people. For my GCSE English oral paper, I'd been so terrified of the practical exam – giving a *prepared* presentation to my class, a class that was largely made up of people who were my friends – that during the mock exam I'd exaggerated the seriousness of a small blow to the head I'd received during rugby training. As I lay in the sanatorium knowing that I was getting away with faking a head injury, I felt ashamed of myself. I knew I could have walked into my class and made my presentation, but I was so fearful of it going wrong that I *faked* concussion. That's pretty bad, isn't it?

If my sixteen-year-old self could see me now, speaking confidently to large groups of complete strangers every few weeks for the last eight years, he would probably fall over with shock. I still get nervous before every single talk I give (sometimes, in the days before or on the morning itself, I think about all sorts of excuses why I can't go), but unless I am genuinely unwell or unable to get there, I will overcome that fear of failure and go through with the talk. If I do fail, if at one of my talks something doesn't work, I know that afterwards I'll think through what went wrong, figure out how I might change things, either practically or in terms of my attitude, to make it work better the next time. I now know that a setback is a chance to improve, to make positive change. Any minor failure is just an indication of something to work on in the future.

One of the ways I have faced the challenge of setbacks – or rather, seen beyond the inevitability of setback – is through the security of routine. The logistics of my daily life are complicated, but if I know my mum, my carer and I are sticking to a routine that works, I can feel much calmer and in control of the process. A good, reliable, workable routine can get you through the most challenging or changing times. The process of devising a routine that suits your needs can actually be hugely pleasing.

I've always been one for sticking to things that work. There was a period pre-accident when my rugby was going well, but I was still worried about failure. So, in order to feel some element of control, before each game I'd get up early, come downstairs into the lovely silence of the front room, put on the TV while I ran through a few exercises and stretches, the same time, the same workout, each week. The plan worked; not only did it help me warm up, it also cleared my mind and made me focus on the match ahead.

There's a saying in sport – control the controllable – which makes perfect sense to me. You look at what you *can* control, put aside the externalities you can't control and drill down into what enables you to manage the situation you are facing. For me, being in control of my nerves or anxiety is key. Whenever I go out to give a talk, I stick to a routine that works for me. I've found keeping to my routine allows me to settle quickly into the unfamiliar place I'm visiting; sometimes I can even relax enough to enjoy the experience.

My routine goes something like this: around two weeks before the talk, I check out the facilities – usually by speaking to someone over the phone, or checking out the venue. I need good access, obviously; a dignified way on to the stage if there is one; and to be absolutely certain they have, or can get in, the right electronic equipment for my PowerPoint presentation to work. I find that people are incredibly receptive; provided they know in advance what I need, they will bend over backwards to accommodate me. The needs of someone in a wheelchair are totally obvious to me now that my eyes have been opened, but it's not automatically obvious to everyone else. I can't assume they will know what is necessary, beyond a certain basic level. I find that if I'm polite and articulate clearly what it is I require, that will achieve much more than a huffy approach in which I assume a sort of entitlement just because I'm disabled. In my experience, people want to help. When polite guidance is offered, they are grateful to have it.

Next, I make sure the clothes I'm going to wear are clean, presentable and set aside for the day of the talk. I wear the same clothes for each talk, so I know my body will be at an optimal temperature. Then, I plan the timings of the day – when we need to leave, when we need to start getting into the car, how long the journey will take, etc. The days are long gone when I could just hop into the back of the car a couple of seconds before leaving.

Those are the things I do well in advance of the day itself. The night before a talk, when I go up to bed I ask my carer to get out my laptop and place it on the chest of drawers in my room in the same spot 'as always'. In the morning, when she comes in to get me up, I ask her to put my laptop on charge. I won't do this the night before because I did it in the morning the first time I did a talk and that's how it will stay forever. Similarly, I won't have it put anywhere else other than on the same chest of drawers. Once I'm ready to go downstairs, I eat the same breakfast. Then, give or take a little more preparation, I am ready to go.

Superstitious? Nah. Just routinitious. As rigid or bonkers as it may seem – would the day *really* go any differently if I had toast instead of porridge? – knowing I've stuck to what I believe works for me seems to help. Even though I'm going out to different places, to talk to different groups of people, and none of that is predictable, imposing order on the things I can manage allows me to be calm, focused and optimistic about the day ahead.

It doesn't always work out as planned. Recently, I was due to give a talk at a women's prison. I was already nervous about going to a venue I'd never been to before, worried about how much they actually wanted to hear me speak, so it unsettled me when we discovered a few days before that the car we usually use was in the garage and unavailable. Mum went to have a look at a hire car to check the doors would be big enough to get my wheelchair in and came back reporting the one she'd chosen would do the job. But on the morning of the talk, that car wasn't available. She called to tell me this and my immediate thought was, no: I don't want to do this talk, I'm not going to do it.

Whenever I think that – I can still get cold feet (well, not that I can feel if my feet are cold) despite being used to giving talks by now – I remind myself of the trouble others have gone to in booking me to speak. I think of the audience. It's not that I think they need to hear my talk, or that their day will be better for it, but I think about letting people down. I wouldn't want to be thought of as someone who disappoints or is seen as flaky.

So, I gritted my teeth and told Mum we'd manage with the hire car she was driving home. It turned out the chair wouldn't fit into the boot, so Mum and my carer had to get it on to the back seat – which wasn't easy as it was a two-door car. The only place it would go was behind my seat at the front, so it was pushing me forward the whole journey. As we drove to the prison I could feel the tension mounting, travelling up my shoulders, invading my mind. When this happens, I tend to react in one of two ways – either I get short with the people I'm around or I go very quiet. Because I knew this was also a tense situation for Mum and my carer, I closed in on myself, trying to focus on the talk ahead.

Arriving at the prison, I was greeted in such a friendly way that I managed a smile. But then, at about two feet off the ground, the lift got stuck. Nothing we could do would make it move. My carer managed to attract attention and someone literally hand-cranked it down. It took ages. But you know what? By this time, so much hadn't gone according to my routine, I kind of relaxed into it. The car hadn't been the usual one and it had been too small, but we'd still got there; I'd been stuck in a lift and I'd got out. What else could go wrong?

Ironically, the talk turned out to be one of the best experiences I've ever had. The women were so welcoming, the atmosphere was brilliant and they asked so many questions. When I came home I was exhausted but strangely exhilarated. A few years ago I would have seen all the obstacles before that talk as setbacks. The moment I'd known our car wasn't going to be ready, I'd probably have cancelled. But that talk was such a great experience that I'm glad I didn't miss it. That experience made me see I can be a bit more adaptable, try to go with the flow. It's not my natural state of being, but ten years down the line I'm still learning. I'm making progress when it comes to being out of my comfort zone. Thanks to a small hire car and an ancient prison lift, I know I don't need to adhere totally to my routine in order to perform well.

Of course, some setbacks have nothing at all to do with my accident or its after-effects. I'm as prone to life's everyday setbacks, such as rejection or work frustrations, as anyone else. I deal with them just like anyone else. I can be disappointed, angry, resigned or stubborn, wait them out, talk them out, accept them for what they are, then move on. I wouldn't claim to have any greater insights in these matters than anyone else. But, if we're talking physical setbacks, such as being ill with a virus or stretching myself too far, then I think I probably do take longer to recover, so I'm more mindful of the need to manage the way I respond. I've learned that the answer to any of these sorts of setbacks lies in one simple four-letter word: rest.

After I worked tremendously hard in all aspects of my physio so that I was able, with the help of e-motion wheels, to use my shoulders to push myself out of Stoke Mandeville, I went back to school to complete my A levels. Then I came home, concentrated on intense physio, started speaking in public, painting, and then decided to write a book. When I look back at this time, I see that I was on this relentless trajectory of pushing myself to achieve more and more. My whole sense of self had been shattered by my accident and it took years to put that back together again. I had this need to prove I could not only achieve but go beyond expectations. This turned out to be incredibly positive in that I did get a lot done, which meant I felt excited by my new life and all the possibilities that lay ahead.

But looking back on those early days I can see that I wasn't being kind to myself. I was pushing my body, sometimes to the point of exhaustion. Inevitably there'd come a point where I'd be unable to do the things I'd set out to do. I'd have to cancel talks, or stop painting or postpone physio. There were times I was so tired that I'd have to spend a few days in bed, which in turn meant it was harder to get back to the place I'd been a few days before. I can see now that I was creating my own series of self-induced setbacks – soldiering on, ignoring any warning signs of fatigue or sickness, even though I knew I was going to suffer down the line.

These days, with the benefit of experience and the great revelation of the power of rest, I know that ignoring physical setbacks can have long-lasting effects. At the first warning signs, I start taking pre-cautions: dosing myself with necessary medication, getting more rest or rearranging talks. In fact, because I suffer during the cold weather, I now tend not to give any talks between November and March; instead I concentrate on other work and challenges.

I can't overstate the power of rest. It's a kindness that only you can gift to yourself; no one else can judge how much you need, and no one else can rest for you. Taking time out, taking *control* of taking time out – from your recovery, from your ambitions, from yourself even – is vital. Rest is not giving up, it's not admitting defeat. It's giving yourself over for a bit of TLC. If you can balance all the things you want to achieve with getting enough rest, then you should be doing OK. It's like an equation: progress + rest = getting-it-about-right. And I know how hard it can be to push yourself to rest.

Every so often I just do nothing. By nothing, I mean planning a day in which I give myself permission to not paint, to not prepare a talk, to not go on social media, to close down on the world outside. Instead, I clear my mind by sleeping, reading or watching films, especially ones I've seen many times over. I find that comforting. It may be different things for you – a lovely long leisurely walk or looking at some of the brilliant forums that chart or share how people with similar challenges are coping. These can be so helpful and affirming, as well as being a good way to interact with others who may be experiencing similar changes to you in their lives.

Recognising our limits is hard to do, especially in a world that encourages us to push beyond them and keep achieving, growing, winning. But we get strong signals – especially from our bodies – when we push ourselves too far. All of us need to learn how to look after ourselves the way we would look after someone else. If our friend looked tired or stressed we wouldn't tell them to keep working through the night, but we might force ourselves to do it. Ask yourself whether you are pushing yourself too hard, or whether you need to back off a little in order to win the long game.

Sometimes, when my mind is clear from resting, I like to reflect. I find these periods of rest expand my thinking. It might be that I have thought of a new or better way to manage some part of my care, or something new to write into my talk, so I record these thoughts into my phone. I don't always listen back, but I find that the process itself has been immensely helpful over the years. I discovered this some time ago when I was thinking about how I'd express my 'story' on my website. Before editing it into something coherent, I just recorded what had happened to me. The process was such a release, it was as if telling my story out loud helped me to let go of the trauma of it. Over the years I've continued to record things on my phone; there's no doubt this has helped me to gain perspective on both practical matters, like knowing what to tell new carers, and emotional matters, such as how I deal with setbacks. It's a great way of understanding yourself over time.

No matter how well we look after ourselves with rest, routine and the support of those around us, we are bound to face setbacks along the way. Some of these we can anticipate, but that doesn't always make them easier to deal with. Some we can't see coming, forcing us to react in the moment. But, as I hope I've shown, we *can* be in control of how we face our setbacks – often our attitude is the only thing we can control when life is difficult. I find when I'm facing something daunting, it is helpful to remind myself of how I've dealt with previous blows. Knowing that I can recover from those gives me the confidence to keep going. From my experience, it's about being robust enough emotionally and prepared enough practically to withstand the entire force of a setback, or at least elements of it. When you need to stop fighting it and just rest, do it. Rest is part of your recovery too.

8

Who and what inspires you?

WHEN I WAS first asked this question I panicked slightly. For a moment or so, I felt compelled to answer with some dazzling, large-scale reply. To pick someone or something that would impress the audience and show me to have been knocked out by great brilliance, fortitude and achievement. Quick, I thought. Name a towering world figure who has inspired millions. Nelson Mandela. Mother Teresa. Their struggles, their lives, the way they overcame adversity, or helped others overcome adversity; the way they stuck to their principles without ever compromising themselves – they've inspired me, right? I looked out into the audience.

'My physio, Ruth,' I said, 'and her amazing "can-do" attitude.'

Then I proceeded to explain why.

Ruth was my physio for just over three years. I'd started working with her during my short visits home from the hospital and continued when I returned full-time. When I look back, those early days after I was discharged were strange. There was this sense of euphoria that I had pushed myself out of the hospital, I'd made it home. But there was a certain bleakness too. This was it: my situation was suddenly very, very real. This was me, in a wheelchair, dependent, for the rest of my life. No matter what I did or thought or felt, here I was, here we were. Life as we had known it was never going to be the same again.

Adjusting to this situation took a great deal of emotional and practical effort. While we all had to figure the best way to get through each day, inevitably we looked to others for guidance and help. Enter Ruth. She's this formidable bundle of energy and expertise, who completely revolutionised not only my physical recovery but the way my family 'handled' me. We soon realised that, regardless how fazed we might be by adjusting to my return home, not to mention my disability itself, Ruth was completely on top of it. She'd seen it all before, had developed her own effective, tried-and-tested methods of exercise and movement. Just as importantly, she instinctively understood the best way to communicate with my family. She was clear, direct, matter-of-fact. While it might not always have been present on the surface – there was, after all, work to be done – her approach was built from a foundation of compassion and empathy. I felt so motivated by the way she explained things to me. Her methods made sense; I understood not just that I needed to do the exercises but why I needed to do them. I was so grateful for her total belief in me every step of the way. She pushed me, she pushed my family too – and I was deeply appreciative that she included them in my recovery.

While she concentrated on building my physical strength, she was also working on my mental and emotional state. The more I could do, the better I felt physically. The better I felt physically, the stronger I felt mentally. In between visits, I was motivated to do all the work that she set me. Our new exercises included the crucial act of balancing. She'd put a rope or bandage round my back and under my arms, then she'd stand in front of me. My carer would cross my legs for me and sit me up, while Ruth would stand in front holding the bandage or rope or band or whatever, so she was taking my weight. At the same time she'd be moving me, helping me to move side to side or forward and back. Gradually we built up so we were doing that without the rope, until I'd be sitting there without anyone touching me – balancing all by myself. This was revolutionary stuff for me at the time. Tough as the physio was, far from dreading her visits, I looked forward to them. Looking back, I can see just how much she helped and understood me. Ruth was an inspiration to me and my family, and I attribute a lot of my optimism, motivation and progress in general to her.

One of the most insightful things she advised was that, once we'd finished working together, rather than continuing with another physiotherapist, I would be better off having a personal trainer. She felt a personal trainer wouldn't be restricted by the confines of the physiotherapy profession and would instead give me a more normal exercise routine, which in turn would be of long-lasting benefit. When we found my PT, Dan, he worked alongside Ruth for a while so he could get used to my body, with her guiding him in how it worked. He had never done anything like this before, but Ruth's attitude as well as her skill were inspirational. She was impressed with his training philosophy of making someone's body function the best way it can. Over the last seven years, Dan and I have achieved some incredible stuff together. We have made amazing progress on my ability to balance, at first building on what Ruth had taught us with me trying to move myself side to side, forward and back. We built it up until we got to the point where Dan put the back of the bed up so I was sitting leaning against the bed, then I had to bring myself forward, using my head and shoulders. Stopping myself from going too far forward by correcting and adjusting myself took monumental effort, but over time we built it up until I could balance, then move myself from side to side. Most people tend to look at their physio or their personal trainer as a person they have to see to get better, or fitter or healthier – as a chore or an expense rather than an inspiration. But I see mine as true inspiration. And always will.

So, while of course I've been inspired by the lives of the great and the good – how can we not be? – in choosing Ruth as my answer the first time I was asked that question, you can see how it's often those closest to us that provide us with the inspiration we need to get through challenging situations. Sure, I could have said that the way Nelson Mandela showed so much dignity and courage while he was locked up on Robben Island inspired me to overcome feelings of self-pity and despair when I was at my lowest in hospital. But that would be a massive exaggeration. The truth is I didn't conjure the inspiration of Nelson Mandela to get me through those dark days. It was the love and support and presence of my family; the unconditional care of the medical team around me, particularly the nurses who worked long, relentless shifts yet were always so kind to me; the gentle but firm direction of my physios, Scott and Frances. They were the ones who inspired me to accept, adapt and move on with the challenges ahead. This may sound cheesy, but I've had enough time to consider my answer and it's the honest truth.

You, too, may find the greatest sources of inspiration in those around you. If you are fortunate enough to have a supportive family, group of friends and a medical team, then make sure you allow yourself to take in all the millions of little things that are inspiring you. It's those glimpses of light along the way that make all the difference. If, on the other hand, you are taking care of a loved one, then know that, however hard it might be, the power you have summoned within you to not only put one foot in front of the other to get through the days, but the love, care, comfort and guidance you are showing them will be inspirational now and going forward. If one definition of inspiration is an individual that people admire and want to be like, then who wouldn't want to be like my mum, dad and my brothers, whose love and care, and the way they adapted to my situation, made life so much more bearable for me, even when things looked so dark.

None of this is to say that we can't be inspired by world-leading heroes, or draw motivation from their stories. In our lives, there are people 'out there', people who we don't personally know, who we admire and want to be like. People we look to when it's a struggle to rise to new challenges. There is no doubt that, looking outwards from the many people close to me who were keeping me together through their everyday presence, the figure who has most inspired me during my recovery is the former England Under-21 rugby player, Matt Hampson.

During a training session in 2005 when Matt was twenty years old, a scrum collapsed on top of him and his spinal cord was severed. Like me, from the moment of his accident, Matt was paralysed from the neck down, but unlike me, he was totally dependent on a ventilator to breathe for him. I was around thirteen when I read about him in the Saracen's club programme. Probably like every other rugby fan, I shuddered and thought, Wow, that's a hell of a thing, maybe I should be a little more careful at my next training session.

One of my rugby coaches knew Matt. When I was in intensive care, even though I wasn't aware of too much going on around me, I was made up when one day he brought me a message from Matt himself. Matt had told my coach that, while he knew it was early days for me, if I ever needed to talk to him or needed anything, he was there. I should 'just feel free to call'.

This was such great a boost. Knowing that someone who had experienced the same life-changing situation had been thinking of me – someone who had got through the initial hurdles that I was now facing – and was offering his support. That message shone a light of hope that has always stayed with me. When I actually got to meet him, about ten months after my accident, and saw for myself how normal his life was despite his dependency, how much he was achieving through his Foundation, I thought he was so awesome I wanted to be like him. He inspired me to realise that I, too, could live my life to the fullest, whatever that was going to be.

Matt continues to inspire me and millions of others. The Foundation he set up provides relief or treatment for anyone who has suffered serious injury or disability, particularly if it was caused by participation in sport or training. In 2011 I became the first beneficiary of Matt's Foundation, receiving a manual cross trainer that I could use to work on my joints, with the help of Ruth and one of my carers, while in a standing position. Much to my surprise, I was then asked to become an official representative of the Foundation, which I was incredibly honoured to accept. My main duties were to talk to or visit young men and women, offering advice and support based on my own experiences.

Meeting Matt literally changed my life. I met him at just the right time in my recovery; his insight, gentle guidance and firm support allowed me to shift my thinking about dependency and how I could live my life going forward.

From time to time, there may be people in the news whose story will touch you, making you see things in a new way. You may remember the story of Tony Nicklinson. Following a stroke, he was struck by locked-in syndrome, which meant, apart from blinking his eyes, he was totally paralysed in every respect. He couldn't move, breathe, swallow or speak. But his mind was aware of everything and his condition was not terminal. He described his life as a 'living nightmare' and made it clear to his family that he wished to die. He had asked the courts to rule that any doctor who helped him end his life should not be charged with murder, arguing that to die was a matter of private autonomy and should not be hindered by law. The court ruled against his request. He refused to eat, and eventually died after contracting pneumonia, which his body was unable to fight.

Tony was an amazing man. He fought for the right to die and he was an inspiration to many. To me though, it was his family who were the inspiration. His wife Jane and his two daughters, Lauren and Beth, were so strong, so supportive, fighting alongside him for his wish to determine his future, to have 'a pain-free and peaceful death'. Their view that life should be about quality and happiness, not 'just for the sake of it' struck a chord with me. Having experienced the support of my family in the most difficult of times, knowing that Tony's were supporting him in choosing death, made me understand this must have been the most painful, brutal experience. To understand and respect your loved one so deeply, to care for them so much that you would *campaign* with them for the right to die, is almost beyond belief.

Since I became visible on social media – especially following the publication of *The Little Big Things* – I have been touched by the many people who have written to me sharing their stories about the ways they, or those close to them, have overcome adversity. It's been a surprise to discover how my story has inspired them, particularly my optimism. I'm not going to lie – it's flattering. Sometimes I can see my own story from an outsider's perspective and reflect on it, hoping that I may be an inspiration for someone else who finds themselves in a similar situation. There is no substitute for someone who has shared the same experience as you, especially when you feel intensely alone in your suffering. I have found so much support and inspiration in the stories of those who have used their pain to help others. I have learned that communities exist that can help support you. If you are struggling, I urge you to find others who may be a little further along the same journey that you are on. Things can feel very bleak in the days immediately following a traumatic incident, whether that's an accident or a diagnosis or bereavement or even a break-up. But there is support out there; when you feel strong enough, I urge you to find it.

9

What does painting mean to you?

LIKE A PAINTING itself, the answer to this question has many layers. Aside from being continually astonished that people like my paintings and want to own them, being able to paint gives me a sense of freedom. There's also a great deal of satisfaction in having accomplished something that accepts yet at the same time goes beyond my disability.

I loved art as a child and spent hours drawing, but as sport took over as my primary interest, I did less of it. At school, the limitations of GCSE and AS level art made me strangely less creative. By the time of my accident, I had lost my enthusiasm altogether. Rediscovering painting when I was bored, confined to bed because of a persistent bedsore on my back, was a massive boost to me. I often wonder whether, if I hadn't found a drawing app on my iPad, I'd be answering a question about my art right now.

Reconnecting with painting gave me an opportunity to discover a tenacious, determined side of myself. It also challenged my levels of patience as I grappled first with drawing on my iPad with a mouth stick, then graduating to an easel using a paintbrush in my mouth. At the beginning, I would veer from intense perseverance to intense irritation at myself or the equipment. But as my attempts took shape, drawing a positive response first from my family, then on social media, I became more confident. My progress was incremental, but with practice I was able to relax into actually enjoying it. The more I did, the more proficient I became, until I reached the point I was sometimes surprised and pleased by the outcome.

I liked the sense of purpose art was giving me. I liked the idea that I had metaphorically taken a deep breath, aware on maybe some unconscious level that this was an opportunity to get something positive out of my new situation. There was also a grim satisfaction that, in the absence of movement in my arms, I could paint using my mouth. There had been a few exhibitions by mouth artists at Stoke Mandeville; when I was there, we'd marvelled at the skill and the sheer tenacity involved in 'doing that'. Now, here I was, struggling, showing rudimentary skill perhaps, but spurred on by the feeling I was achieving something. There is a real beginning and end in painting; I liked the sense of completion that finishing gave me, even if I knew I had a long way to go in becoming as good as some of the artists we'd admired.

Painting definitely took me 'out of myself', giving me time and space to concentrate on something outside of my immediate situation: my recovery, my dependence, the many vast changes I was coming to terms with. Whatever challenges you are facing, if you can find a form of escape that does the same for you, I can almost guarantee it will give you respite from your situation. Getting outside the realities of day-to-day coping makes you feel better about yourself, which in turn can help with shifts in perspective, the way others relate to you and your sense of what may be possible. Once again it was the more positive side of my circumstances that forced me to look at what I could do, rather than what I couldn't do.

As I developed my skills – moving to the easel and painting on canvas – I started to get some commissions. These were mostly from friends and family, but they were still real orders that, once accepted, I had to fulfil. My dad helped me order in new materials so I could experiment with different paints and backgrounds. Before I knew it, my hobby had become more serious than I'd ever intended. It meant a great deal to me that my art was – and hopefully still is – on the walls in houses and offices all over the place. I enjoyed the interaction with people that came with commissions, listening to the story behind the images they wanted painting, their reasons for asking me to do it. I did have to get used to the pressure that a commission puts you under. It's one thing producing a painting for my own satisfaction – I could be happy with the practice even if the result wasn't great – but it would be a different thing altogether to screw up someone's treasured request for which they are paying good money.

In October 2015 I was asked if I wanted to exhibit some of my paintings at my old school. I was nervous about this because it meant producing several pieces by a certain date, which stirred up those old feelings of not wanting to accept in case I failed. But something inside told me to accept the challenge. Preparing for the exhibition was stressful, but I managed it. When it came down to it, making a speech, talking in public (this was in the days before I'd ventured into giving talks) as I introduced the exhibition turned out to be far more stressful than painting to a deadline.

Painting gives me choice. I have the freedom to paint what I like, how I like. While I'm now at the stage where I've developed a style and technique, I still like to push myself to try out new things – more detailed compositions or complicated colour combinations. Setting myself new challenges, even in something I am doing regularly, is invigorating. It also gives me a thrill of achievement when I pull it off.

I'd always recommend looking to new horizons in whatever it is you are striving for. Don't push yourself unrealistically; just thinking of new ways to enliven old or existing habits or patterns can be very refreshing.

There have been times when producing paintings to commission or getting the numbers needed for an exhibition has caused me undue stress or physical exhaustion. Painting can take its toll on my body, especially on my neck and shoulders. I have struggled my way through some of my commissions to the detriment of my mental and physical health. But that can be a lesson in itself: it's taught me to recognise when I need to rest.

The picture you see on the cover of this book is perhaps the best example of this. I get my inspiration for paintings from all sorts of places; this one came from a documentary on Everest. As I was watching, I was struck by the beauty of the glow cast by the low sun over the mountains. It was one of those moments that moved me to try to capture it in a painting. It was quite early on in the process for me, so I was still grappling with techniques, but with my post-accident 'can-do' attitude in place, I thought I would give it a go.

As I thought about how I would depict the image that had so taken me, I prepared my paints. I was still painting on white backgrounds, so I knew I'd have to paint everything including the sky. Little did I know how difficult this would be. It took me four five-hour days to complete. For large parts of each day I was enjoying the challenge, even the act of painting all the little black lines that demanded precision and texture. But I just couldn't get the sky right. As that had been the element of the composition that had so drawn me to the mountain itself, this mattered to me. So I kept pushing myself – too hard.

By the last day I was absolutely shattered. The tops of my shoulders and back of my neck felt shredded. My breathing had also been affected by all the fine lines I'd been painting – holding the paintbrush in my mouth for sustained periods meant I had to hold my breath. Over the four days, this became uncomfortable, to say the least. As I painted the last stroke, then took a look at the completed picture, I felt satisfied I'd captured a little of what I'd seen in the documentary, but I was so out of it, I had to spend the weekend in complete recovery mode. It wasn't until a few days later that I felt human again, though the knock-on effects of over-exerting myself reverberated throughout the rest of that week.

I'd got to the top of the mountain, so to speak, but on the way up – and down – I'd learned a big lesson. In retrospect, it was a lesson I badly needed to learn: pushing myself unnecessarily outside my comfort zone was not a good idea. If I was feeling tired while painting, or doing anything else that made demands on me, I had to listen to my body. To push on through for the sake of it was stupid. The experience taught me that, when it came to painting, I was the boss. I was in control of my timetable – if I failed to maintain that control, it was down to me to manage expectations better. When working on commissions, this might mean moving the delivery date, but the expectations I was heaping on myself were sometimes much harder to manage than those of clients.

I did learn from this and have adjusted my behaviour accordingly. In the same way that I no longer commit to giving talks in the winter because it's

harder for me to get about, I won't accept commissions unless I know I have the time and headspace
and energy to paint to order. When I do, just like any
other freelancer, I give myself realistic deadlines. If in
the course of doing the painting this changes for some
reason, I make sure to tell the client the painting will
be a little later. I find that being clear and direct like
this makes a big difference. It's not as if I am doing
open heart surgery; the completion of a painting isn't
a life-or-death situation, but I always make sure that
if the commission is for a special event, there is plenty
of time built in to the timetable. Like anything in life,
clear and honest communication is the best and, in
my opinion, only way to operate.

I don't want to give the impression that painting is
mostly about the physical act for me. The discipline,
focus and thought that goes into each painting is both
enjoyable and challenging. I did a painting I called
The Beached Boat which was the most detailed, fullest
painting I've ever done. The beach itself took two
whole days to complete. It's made up of a series of
scribbles and tiny brush strokes that took a lot of
movement, but was more mentally exhausting than

physical because I had to conceive of ways in which to achieve what I wanted. Similarly, I painted a picture of a family's house in France that took a lot of precise brush work, but it was about producing something the client would both recognise and like that occupied my thoughts as I worked.

I'd be lying if I didn't admit to being flattered that people want to put my paintings on their walls. I used to think it was a bit bonkers; at times I felt I was a fraud in some way – that it was only because of my disability, a sense of marvel that I could hold a paintbrush in my mouth and produce something half decent, that people paid me any attention at all. But now, as I see how my paintings sell at exhibitions and online, how people react to new ones on social media, I feel more confident about my ability. I also like that I create paintings that get a response. This has helped give me the confidence to explore different methods, different materials and more intricate subject matter.

The fact that a couple of my paintings fetched considerable amounts in a charity auction for Matt's Foundation also makes me feel good. It gives me a unique way of contributing to causes I support, and of course it is flattering that someone is prepared to pay through the nose to own one of my pictures. I have, over the years, accepted commissions to help charities. I was made up when I was asked by the Matt Hampson Foundation to paint twelve British sporting icons, including Jessica Ennis-Hill and David Beckham, for a 2017 calendar that was sold in branches of Sainsbury's nationwide. I enjoyed doing that – not only the actual paintings but the fact that I could help the Foundation in an effective way. It felt quite surreal to know that my artwork was going to be in shops throughout country.

I love the fact that art can spark different feelings in people. At my exhibitions, I've seen people walk straight past one of my paintings, while others have lingered or started conversations with others who are also looking at it. When you think about it, they are seeing the same painting. A highland cow is a highland cow is a highland cow. But for some it may trigger some memory or other, some fondness for cows or the countryside, while others may simply respond to the image. I like to write something about why I chose to paint each of my pictures in the hope that chimes with people. Take ,*The Highland Cow*. I wanted to express my fascination with these animals; despite the fact you rarely see their expressions, their faces convey so much character. While I was faithful to the long face-covering hair of the cow, I chose to leave one eye exposed and the tongue sticking out so I could show what I consider to be an endearing, playful nature.

People always ask me which of my paintings are the most popular. I suppose they mean which ones sell the most, or which get the most likes on social media. However I measure this, it's always surprising to me which of my paintings seem to capture people's imagin-ation. When I was drawing on the iPad, my depiction of Audrey Hepburn was very popular. On canvas, my most popular painting is probably the colourful stag with pink antlers. It's funny because on the first day I was painting this, I thought it was rubbish. On the second day, I ended up taking most of the colour off and replacing it with black paint. I'd lost heart and was five minutes from binning it, but as always when I get to that point, I try looking for solutions, even if later they don't work. Two days of painting may not seem like a long time, but I knew I'd regret it if I didn't have one last try. Since I had a load of pink paint mixed, I thought: I've nothing to lose. So I painted the antlers. When I'd finished, I thought they looked quite cool. The next morning when I looked at it, I decided I really liked it, so I went ahead and posted it.

What do I know? It turned out to be one of the most popular I'd ever done, getting thousands of retweets and likes. I still get a lot of orders for the print. Whenever I look at it now, it reminds me that giving up is a bad idea; experimenting can lead to unexpectedly successful results. I suppose painting being a bit of a metaphor for other aspects of my life is another alluring thing about it. It's like a microcosm of the bigger things I face. It has helped me confront my old habits of not trying in case of failure. First, there isn't any such thing as failing in painting – well, unless you literally throw away the painting before it's finished. Even if I don't particularly like the finished result of a painting I've done, I still get satisfaction out of persevering and trying something new.

I am also often asked which of my paintings is my favourite. My answer can vary. Sometimes it's obvious to me that it's one of my more 'successful' pieces, while at other times, I might have been looking through some of my old paintings and been taken back to specific memories of when I painted them, which for some reason can make one of them a favourite in a nostalgic sort of way. But I do have some perennial favourites which include *The Highland Cow* with the floppy hair; the first black-and-white lion that I ever did – *King of the Jungle* – because I felt I'd got something right in the majesty of its profile; *The Beached Boat* because it was hard to pull off, I had to work very hard on the underside of the boat and the beach was made up of about a thousand different strokes. Finally, *The Chickens* because these are the chickens we have at home and I wanted to capture their different personalities, which I hope I did. I also worked out different techniques for size and perspective on this painting which I have used in subsequent ones.

Painting means so much to me for a number of reasons. I guess the main reason is that, alongside public speaking, it epitomises my belief that adversity has given me a gift. While I may not be able to use my hands to do anything, I have worked hard and adapted to be able to use my mouth. If I say so myself, sometimes the results are quite good.

In the early days after a major life-change, it may be hard to imagine that adversity might bring gifts in its wake. Of course no one should feel pushed into finding the silver lining when they are still facing up to a changed reality. In my experience, this is something that only comes with time; ten years after my accident, I am able to recognise it. When you are ready, I hope that you will discover gifts of your own, and that they will bring to you the satisfaction and sense of achievement that painting has brought to me.

10

What are your goals going forward?

LIKE A LOT of people, I'm energised by new projects, new challenges, and I've realised that I have to keep moving the goalposts to stay motivated. For the first few years after my accident, once I'd got used to being disabled, I was absorbed in consolidating the ambitions I had started out with: adapting to my new situation, pushing myself to speak in public, working on my art. Giving talks and painting are still very much part of my life, but in the past two or three years, I have set myself new horizons to keep things fresh.

One of those – perhaps the most important for me personally – is to move away from home so I can live independently from my parents. Of course, I will need twenty-four-hour care for the rest of my life, but this does not limit my independence. If that sounds like a complete contradiction, let me explain.

I'm twenty-eight years old. Like everyone I know of my age, I need my own, independent living space. Don't get me wrong. I love my mum and dad, and we've been through more than most together. But knocking on thirty and still sharing a house with your parents? Well, it's not a great place to be for a young guy, no matter what his situation. And that's without the added complications of carers and the sort of disability I have. Up to now, it's been brilliant living here; it's worked out well. It's been a great source of comfort, living in close proximity to my parents – physically and emotionally. Not having to worry about the everyday demands of running a home has allowed me to focus on getting used to the life I am living post-accident.

My friends have mostly moved out of their childhood homes and are living with other friends or their partners. When I go round to see them, I find myself a little envious. Not because they are able-bodied – this is something I'm long over – but because of their independent set-ups and not having their parents around all the time. When my friends come here, my parents always give us space and don't expect to join in, but the very fact they are *around* can make me feel like I'm fourteen all over again. Over the past couple of years, I have felt a creeping sense of infantilisation just by virtue of still being at home. Sometimes I wonder if living with my parents has also made me a little too comfortable. The thing is, I don't bear much *responsibility*. Nor do I have full control over my environment, and that's something I would now like to have.

It's good to identify places in our lives where we may have, often without noticing, fallen into the embrace of the comfort zone against our own best interests. Certainly, immediately following a catastrophic event, it's understandable to make comfort and security your priority. But as you move on in life, adapting to changed circumstances, it's been my experience that you need to push yourself to let go of some of those security blankets in order to keep on growing.

So. My next goal is to build a house of my own. Or, rather plan, finance, oversee and manage the building of a house for myself (and my carers). I know that sounds very ambitious, but I need a new challenge, something that pushes me outside my comfortable comfort zone, and this seems just the thing. I needed a goal that would make demands of me. Something I have no experience in, so I can learn on the job. Something that, to be honest, I have no idea how to do. Of course, the finished house will also result in me moving out and living independently.

Before you say anything, yes, I do know that anything to do with houses can be – will be – stressful. I know that while it's being built I'll have to make a million choices about things I've never even considered need considering. When I'm buried under catalogues of door handles or bathroom accessories, I may well wish I'd never even had one negative thought about living at home. But all that is yet to come. For now, though I'm aware of the pitfalls, even those are a part of pushing myself that appeals to me. It would be all too easy in my situation to allow others to make decisions for me. I could make excuses for myself, and who would blame me? But that is not who I am, or who I want to be. I know that independence means making these choices for myself, even when they're annoying or demanding. While I know that things will be uncertain, that not everything will work out quite as I envisage, I also know that if I don't try I'll never know.

I've already progressed a long way with plans for my new home. In fact, building is due to begin very soon. When I first realised I'd saved enough for a deposit, and moving out could be a reality, I looked at loads of small houses near to my parents. I want to move out, but I don't want to move *too* far away. At last I found one close by that I knew I could modernise.

One of my aims is to make my house completely adaptable to disabled living – for me; and able-bodied living – for my carers. I also want to make it as sustainable and environmentally friendly as possible. This kind of challenge, one that is in touch with my ambitions as well as my principles, fires me up. I am now working with the same architects who, when I came back permanently from Stoke Mandeville, put a lift in the house and rearranged the layout upstairs, widening doors for my wheelchair, designing new floors and a wet room for me. They had some great insights and were extremely skilled at making adjustments that made a difference to my daily life. They also helped me navigate the tricky path of planning permission, neighbours and council guidelines. We had to convene a meeting to discuss the plans with the neighbours as there will be a fair amount of rebuilding and reimagining the existing house. Although I'm used to speaking to big rooms of people, I was very nervous when it came to being in a room with the neighbours; if they'd had serious objections it would have meant my house couldn't go ahead. Luckily, they were understanding about the need for the work, and we got the green light.

I have come to discover that designing a house from scratch is very satisfying, especially for someone like me who likes to have control over their environment. I know it's a bit of an extreme way to get a place that works perfectly for you, and not everyone has that luxury, but it's just a bigger example of something I have always known: after a life-changing event like my accident, when everything has been turned on its head, having some control over any part of your life that you can is vital if you're to stay sane.

On a smaller scale, this is true of my current bedroom in my parents' home. Whereas you might just see a bedroom with regular things in it, if I were to talk you through why things are where they are, or why the things that are there are there, you would soon see that I know exactly what's where and why it is there and what I need it for, or want it there for. You would understand why I'm not best pleased if anyone takes something away or switches things around without me knowing. We sometimes criticise people as 'control freaks' for needing their environment to be 'just so', but when we understand why someone might be controlling, and what their specific needs are, we begin to understand their behaviour and judge it less harshly. It's especially important for those of us who have been forced to accept a lack of control in other areas of our lives.

Moving out and living by myself needs careful planning. For a start, without the daily support of my parents, I'll need two full-time live-in carers. Making the available space work best for a house of three people of different needs is something I've enjoyed doing with the architects. I've come to learn that it's not just about what room goes where, but how I want and need to live. For example, it came as a revelation that I don't actually need to have a bedroom upstairs, so I am going to have one downstairs, along with a kitchen, a living area, a specially designed bathroom for me, plus a bedroom with a small bathroom for the carer who is on duty. All the fixtures and fittings will be bespoke, designed for my level of disability – wide doorways, a lower kitchen so I can sit alongside friends and family if they are cooking – but without looking too clinical (I want this to look like a home, not a hospital rehabilitation ward). I'm also going to put in a kitchen, bathroom and living space upstairs for my carers, so they can enjoy a degree of separation from me. If I have friends round, my carers can go upstairs, chill out and cook for themselves, without having to join in with us. There's a garden and we've designed a patio and kept the lawn as low maintenance as possible, with a rainwater retention system that will irrigate the grass. Thinking about these things, prioritising things that will make living as easy as possible for all of us, has been so rewarding. Making decisions has become less stressful as the process has evolved. When I feel bogged down by the endless details, I remember the bigger picture and that motivates me all over again.

I've also been looking into ways of making my home environmentally sustainable. The house has been designed to 'follow the sun', with loads of solar panels retaining energy. The whole place will be airtight, so the specially designed heating system – a life saver for helping me maintain my body temperature – will only need to be run at a low level. One of the things that my family have had to accommodate since my accident is my inability to control my body temperature. I can almost hear their collective sigh of relief when they throw open windows and turn off the heating once I finally move out.

Hopefully, building will have started by the time you are reading this, and I'll still be feeling as excited about all the challenges that lie ahead. Living independently is something I couldn't have dreamed of a few years ago but, bit by bit, I have come to a point where I can now see it as a reality. I am gearing up for the ride, as bumpy as it might be. Since my accident, I know that bumps happen along the way, and as long as I'm mentally prepared for setbacks or things not going quite to plan, I have confidence that the goal I've set myself of designing and building my own house, and moving out of home, is worth pursuing. I am hugely looking forward to the day when I am wheeled through my own front door.

So. That's one clear goal. In other areas of my life, I guess I'm more content to continue with routines, the way things have been, the way they're proven to work. Take physio. While new targets, working up to higher levels of strength, were vital in the early days after my accident, over the last few years it's been about letting progress evolve more naturally. My trainer Dan and I mix up various routines that we've created to keep it interesting; everything we do contributes in some way to me being stronger and more balanced. One of my ongoing goals is to remain in my wheelchair rather than use one with arm and head rests or any electronic devices. For that I need to maintain the strength in my back and shoulders for the rest of my days. Physio is a way of life for me now, but it's more about maintaining levels than always seeking new highs. I don't need to push myself all the time, in everything, and that is another lesson I've learned to take on board.

In my opinion, you don't always need to set hugely ambitious new goals in order to make progress. I prefer sticking to routines, picking challenges that might need loads of focus or energy but are essentially, in themselves, manageable. There have been times when I needed to set myself new goals and rise to meet the challenges that come with that. But, equally, there have been times when maintaining previously set goals has been as effective as thinking up new ones. You don't always have to go big. Achievable, effective goals, however small – just like progress – are the ones that will see you through.

That's not to say you can't also have bigger long-term goals. I do have one that I am thinking of taking on, but at the moment I'm just in the planning stages. One of my ambitions is to speak out more for disability rights, to show that disabled people are able. I'd love to help break down the barriers that still exist between the perception of what life is like for disabled people – essentially *un*able and sad – and the reality – able and positive. I know that I have a lot to say, but equally I know that now it isn't the right time for me to put in all the energy needed to campaign on a public platform. For now, I will continue supporting people who write to me on social media or email to tell me their stories about overcoming adversity and share with them my insight and experience in overcoming traumatic, life-changing events. But in the long term I'm thinking about how I might make a broader contribution. It's good to feel that there are goals to continue working towards, even if I'm not ready for them yet.

Because the other thing I've come to understand is that I am not going anywhere. As far as I know – as far as any of us know – there's plenty of time to achieve the goals I have in mind, and even more time to discover new interests and ambitions. I don't need to be in a tremendous hurry to get to all the things that matter to me. There will be time. Equally, I remain open-minded as to what my goals might be in the future, how different they may look to today. If you'd told sixteen-year-old me that my goal would be to remain strong enough to sit in a non-power-assisted wheelchair, I wouldn't have known what you were talking about. I wanted to be an international rugby superstar. Maybe, in twenty years' time, I'll look back at this moment and think, how did I ever think I would know enough to attempt *that*?

Having gone through a traumatic life-changing event and spent the past ten years adapting to a new way of living, seeing and being, there is one thing I am pretty sure of: life is to be lived and enjoyed in the present. The past has happened; it cannot be changed. The future has not yet happened; when it comes, you may be in a very different place to where you are now. Goals are a good thing to have, but not at the cost of living in the moment.

As Eckhart Tolle wrote in *The Power of Now*: 'Life is now. There was never a time when your life was not now, nor will there ever be.'

So I guess the answer to the question at the start of this chapter is this: living in the present is my goal. Right here and right now.

11

_____

If you were put in charge of improving the daily lives of disabled people, what would you prioritise and why?

THIS IS A question I sometimes get asked when people have heard me say there's a lot of work to be done in improving the lives of disabled people. The truth is, while I have a ton of thoughts on the subject, it would take a lifetime to answer this question fully because it is so complex. To start with, you'd need to have a massive shift in attitudes towards, and perceptions of, disability, the disabled and what it's like to live with disability. Only then can you begin to tackle the practicalities the question implies. Even the term itself, *dis-abled*, is problematic, with its negative implications. When you start from a position that labels you 'less able', it can take massive resilience to see yourself as able or valued. Couple this with the way we are often portrayed as people who don't make a contribution to society – helpless, dependent, generally self-pitying about our disabilities . . . It does not paint a happy picture.

You already know my views. Despite attempts by the media to persuade you otherwise, lots of disabled people lead useful, normal, happy lives, contributing fully to society. Many more disabled people would like to do the same – *yearn* to, in fact – but find themselves unable to lead the fulfilling, varied lives they long for. This might be through lack of support, financial or otherwise, not just in the personal but in the public sphere. The workplace accessibility and flexibility that others take for granted is denied to the disabled. And that's just the beginning.

I'm fortunate to have a social media presence that allows me to challenge untruths and wrongful assumptions about what it is to be disabled. When I do take a stand, I find it gratifying that the response is generally overwhelmingly positive – though heads up to the persistent troll who tells me I must be using my hands to paint and am therefore a total fraud. While the support and comments I receive may be some sort of barometer as to how attitudes are shifting, I never kid myself that it's a fraction of enough.

I have been heartened by the online interest in me as a disabled man, and surprised – astonished, actually – that so many strangers were willing to engage, seeking an insight into how I live my disabled life. Maybe, just maybe, in following the minutiae of parts of my disabled life, I have helped people see what it's like. I hope I may have shone a light on the inequalities and false perceptions of the disabled. Perhaps these strangers have, in turn, shared my experience with others, and that will help with understanding, which may lead to change. Somehow it's easier for people to relate to the personal experience of one individual than to the catch-all general term 'the disabled'. I hope I may also have helped other disabled people along the way by opening up parts of my disability and experience to the scrutiny of others. But I have never kidded myself that I speak for anyone but me, nor that my 'reach' is anything more than a drop in the ocean when it comes to giving disabled people the presence, rights, infrastructure and dignity we deserve.

As I said earlier, when the time is right I would love to campaign more actively and with greater commitment to ensuring total equality for disabled people. Perceptions about us need dragging into the twenty-first century. We deserve to be valued as full members of society. I've already been looking at where my energies might be best placed when it comes to campaigning. I am an all-or-nothing type of person; when I choose to dedicate my time and energy to this work, I will want to give it my full focus. So this is not the right time for that campaigning step, but it motivates me to know the time is coming when I'll give it my all. For now, though, in answer to the question, let me focus on the more practical areas in which I would make improvements to the daily lives of disabled people.

From the moment of being wheeled into hospital after my accident to the present, I have been surrounded by people who in one way or other, either professionally or personally, have experience of living with someone with a disability. In other words, while it took a long time for me and my family to get used to all the changes my disability has entailed, we have come to adapt. We were fortunate in being able to install a lift into the house, to have modifications made to accommodate the path of my wheelchair. We have got the art of sliding me out of my wheelchair into the front passenger seat of the car down to a T. When friends and family come round, or when I go to visit them, everyone is used to accommodating my needs, such as emptying my urine bag or lifting me up or down stairs. I will be making my new house even more disabled-friendly. With the privilege of being able to design my own purpose-built environment from scratch, I'll have the luxury of a homely and practical living space that is built specially for me. I've also been fortunate in having professionals such as carers and physios who are attuned to my needs.

Which is to say I guess in some ways I live in a bubble. It's a bubble of care, of adaptations, of being around people who understand my situation. But. And this is a big but. I realise every day of my life how fortunate I have been not only to have the resources for all this, but also the emotional support of those around me. I'm also acutely aware it is nothing like this when I am out in the real world, trying to live the life of a disabled person in an environment that rarely takes us into consideration.

In 2018, the British disability charity SCOPE did a survey of 2,000 working-age disabled adults. Of those questioned, 49 per cent felt excluded from society; 40 per cent didn't feel valued; 42 per cent did not feel the UK was a 'good place' for disabled people. That's shocking, especially when you consider that this is one of the world's richest countries. A great deal of that sense of exclusion comes down to how we feel we are perceived, which I would argue stems from negative stereotyping of disabled people in the media. The lack of practical adaptations in public facilities also plays its part. These are things that could easily be sorted if there was the will to address the problem in society, in businesses, in government central and local. For that to happen, disabled people need to be given a proper voice and presence in designing public and private spaces.

Don't get me wrong. I'm not moaning or complaining; nor am I saying that there isn't any effort going into making life easier for disabled people. There have been huge improvements over past decades. But even now, in an age of greater transparency and awareness, the provision of, for example, disabled parking bays or ramps or disabled toilets, can feel like little more than lip-service. A local council, or a public building, can claim they've improved access by doing the bare minimum, even though those changes fall short of making it possible for disabled people to use a service or facility with ease and dignity. Until they can enjoy that basic right, we have made no progress worthy of the name.

Take the new cinema complex that's recently opened near me. It's fantastic – twenty screens, restaurants, plenty of car parking spaces, etc. It's been carefully designed, bearing all sorts of needs in mind, and it's proving tremendously popular. So, off we went one weekend to see a film, hopeful that it would be a stress-free, pleasant experience when it came to accessibility, comfort and dignity. Before I tell you why it wasn't, I have to say that the cinema itself was a total pleasure. Because there are so many screens, each one is quite small and there is enough room across all of them to have wheelchair spaces that work, i.e. spaces that aren't necessarily right at the front. This is quite common in cinemas, and as a result I've either had to miss half the film because I've not been able to keep my head back for the duration, or I've strained to watch the whole thing and suffered with terrible neck ache for the rest of the week.

The new complex had ramps for my wheelchair, lifts that worked, and altogether the interior was a disabled-friendly space. But by the time we arrived that day, all of the disabled parking spots had been taken, so we had to park on the other side of the complex. Now, I appreciate this may not feel like a big deal to you. Perhaps you consider this inconvenience to be insignificant in comparison to actually being able to see the film in comfort, but believe me, it isn't. There's a reason disabled people need their bays and it's not just about proximity, though that of course does help.

When I am taken out from the front passenger seat of the car, I have to be put into my wheelchair. We need to open the door as wide as it goes, with enough room between the open door and the next car to be able to put up my wheelchair so I can be placed in it comfortably, without me, or the person putting me in my chair, being in any danger from other vehicles. Car parks are not safe places, so the relative safety of the disabled area is sacrosanct. When we had to park on the other side of the complex, it was tricky, unsafe and frustrating trying to get me out of the car and into my chair. The experience put me on edge and my family in danger. Navigating me and my wheelchair to the main entrance, across the car park, was equally nerve-racking. As a result, we arrived feeling frazzled.

While I bought the tickets – yes, the machines were wheelchair-height friendly – my dad went to look at the disabled parking bays. This is what he discovered. One: despite there being twenty screens with at least two wheelchair-accessible spots per screen and a myriad of restaurants, all wheelchair-accessible, there were only twenty disabled parking bays available. So that's at least forty spaces within the cinema, yet only twenty parking spaces outside. Two: of the twenty cars parked in the disabled bays, only ten had blue disabled badges displayed on the dashboards.

This came as no surprise to me. While increasingly catered for, disability is constantly underprovided for. I'd be a millionaire if I had a pound for all the times I have been to public places where there has only been one toilet for disabled and baby-changing combined, or the only disabled toilet has been out of use because it's being used for storage or it's not been big enough for wheelchairs so has been 'decommissioned until it's fixed'. There have been times when this has meant I've had to have my leg bag emptied under the table in a restaurant. Think about that for a minute. Whoever is with me at the time has had to go under the table to empty my urine, then carry it away to a nearby toilet. Looking past the utter indignity of this for both her and me, there are also hygiene considerations to bear in mind, not to mention a great deal of frustration.

I'd be even richer if I had a penny for every car parked in a disabled parking bay that does not have a blue badge on display. Before you accuse me of being judgemental, I am not saying that all these cars belong to able-bodied people. There may be valid reasons for disabled drivers or those transporting them not to have their blue badges with them that particular day. But I'd be willing to bet these spaces were occupied by people without the necessary parking dispensations for disability, parked there because they were 'just popping in for one second'. Again, I'm not saying all these people are evil monsters, knowingly and deliberately denying disabled people access, but this sort of behaviour shows that we simply aren't at the forefront of people's minds. The assumption is that, because we may not be visible or there aren't that many of us, we don't *need* those spaces. Well, I have news for you. We exist, we are visible if you look, what's more, we do need those spaces. Even if we too are 'just popping in for one second' we need to pop in from the safest, most convenient place possible.

I could go on. I love going to the theatre but the experience of booking tickets or getting suitable 'seats' itself is so stressful, I'm completely put off. Recently I went to see a play at a well-known London theatre. When I called beforehand to tell them I was disabled, they were perfectly pleasant and (on the phone at least) accommodating. But when we arrived, the ramps were too short and too steep, while my 'seat' was at the end of a row in the stalls, thereby blocking all the others in that row, with people having to clamber over me or move my chair to get past. There was just about room for my fairly narrow chair, so anyone in an electric chair or with a headrest would have struggled. The angle of my seat was hopeless too, with a great big pillar taking up a third of my view of the stage. I had to crane my neck to see, which I found intolerable as the show wore on. I loved what I saw of it, but overall, this was a massively disappointing experience which put me off trying again for a while. It's simply too exhausting, too humiliating, too 'other'. It's hard enough getting up to town, so the rest of the outing needs to be straightforward and stress-free – even enjoyable, if that isn't too much to ask.

What frustrates me more than anything are theatre or cinema websites where you can't buy wheelchair seats online. You think, that's impossible, so you keep searching, eventually giving up and calling, only to be told, 'You can't book wheelchair tickets online, you have to call to book them.' This is ridiculous. Firstly, it's harder for me and other disabled people to use the phone than to use a computer (some people can't use the phone at all); secondly, if you are going to make it hard for us, at least let us know on the website so we don't spend hours searching for a facility that isn't there.

On more than one occasion, I've phoned ahead and explained my situation to a manager or member of staff, received a promise that my 'requirements will be met', only to discover on arrival that the establishment does not have the facilities or cannot provide the promised assistance. People want to be helpful, I appreciate that, but they don't fully understand the consequences for a disabled person when they fail to deliver. It's not just an 'inconvenience'. On one occasion, being told by a cinema that a wheelchair seat would be available, I arrived to find that this meant turfing a family off some sofa seats, asking them to help move the sofa to another part of the cinema, finding them other seats, then attempting to slide my wheelchair in so it didn't obscure the view of people behind me (it did). Like most people, I don't want to cause a disruption for others or be treated differently. These experiences have left me feeling embarrassed, 'in the way', a problem to be solved, rather than just another paying customer.

I won't name the theatres or the cinemas because I'm not in the business of shaming. To their credit, they have responded positively to my 'feedback'. The individual staff members could not have been nicer; they were clearly embarrassed at the lack of infrastructure that made it impossible to accommodate me without making me feel self-conscious and 'other'. Fortunately, I have a thick skin that allows me to remain outwardly calm and polite. But inwardly, part of me withers each time I am subjected to this. Along with many other disabled people, each experience leaves me less eager to venture out.

So, what's the answer? I see it as my responsibility to point out the lack of provision or misuse of it – your needs can't be met unless your voice is heard. But I have a life to live, a living to earn, and it could take over my entire life if I were to doggedly follow up every single incidence of poor accessibility until it was improved. I am just one voice. It would be much better for the needs of disabled people to be listened to and acted on as an integral part of the everyday needs of society. Obviously, that means more spaces to cater for more disabled people who want to go to the cinema or have a meal out with friends but may need to park nearer to the venue when they get there. Disabled people need to be invited on to planning committees to ensure our voices are heard and our needs met. Inconsiderate behaviour, such as parking in disabled bays or cramming disabled toilets full of unwanted furniture so they can't be used, can only be addressed by the general population showing some consideration. I find most people want to be helpful, but they seem oblivious to the needs of disabled people. I hope speaking out, as I do here, will go some way to increasing awareness.

Often, solutions to problems of accessibility are simple. Providing a wider ramp is a minor consideration to a venue, for example, but a major one to its disabled customers. There has to be a willingness on the part of non-disabled people to address these needs. I'm not being passive here – as disabled advocates for better access, we can do our part by giving our opinions, sharing our experiences – but meaningful change will require the support of the entire community, disabled and able-bodied.

Sometimes I like to think of practical, technological solutions that haven't yet been invented. An 'oyster card' type system for checking in and out of disabled parking areas? A stair-climbing wheelchair? There are all sorts of innovations that will no doubt transform lives. Maybe, in the not-too-distant future, we won't need disabled parking bays as we will all be transported about the place some other way. I like to think that technology will help us find practical solutions that will make our lives easier.

But for these 'solutions' to mean something beyond the 'problem' that they solve, we will all have to shift our attitude towards disability. Adaptations and access are only the beginning. Society as a whole needs to be more aware of the way disabled people live their lives; to understand that my needs may be different from your needs but they are no less important or significant for that. Like everyone, disabled or not, I want to be valued for who I am. I want to be treated in a way that takes in my disability but also sees beyond it, to everything else that I am, can be and long to be. Just as much as any able-bodied person, I want to enjoy my life. To go to the theatre or the cinema, to a restaurant or hotel, to travel, to work, to contribute, to take an active part in society and be part of the community you inhabit. I want you to know that I don't want to be – and I won't be – shut away. I won't make my disability invisible because it might make you uncomfortable. I want you to talk to me, to ask me questions, questions about my disabled life but also questions about my art, what I think of the England rugby squad, what films I've enjoyed recently.

In other words, I want you to treat me – and every disabled person you ever come across from now on – with the dignity, respect and care that you might show other people in your life. To see me, to hear me and to share a common experience of life with me. That, more than anything, would improve – and transform – my daily life beyond anything practical.

The Power in Us

AT THE END of every talk I give, before the questions begin, I say this: 'I suspect some of you may be thinking that I have been brave, but I don't feel particularly brave. I simply found myself in a particular situation and I responded in the same way I'm sure almost everybody in this room would have reacted. My belief is that this is the human spirit. That's the way we are made.'

These are the words that have remained steadfast in the ten years since my accident and I truly believe in them. I have shown myself, and now hopefully you too, that at our core we are capable of change. We have within us the power to change ourselves and to change how we think. Each one of us is capable of surviving incredibly tough moments, of digging deep, finding the power in us to adapt, to accept our past, to make progress – realistically and with great optimism. Taking on this challenge – facing it instead of hiding from it – is what allows us to live the best lives we can, building on our new circumstances, focusing on the positive opportunities adversity can bring.

If we are realistic and unflinching in facing the future, if we are true to ourselves, if we give ourselves time to adapt and grow, I believe we can all find the power within.